"Finally, a book that really will make you a better and happier person! Every parent and child will treasure Pat and Karyn's rock-solid advice, touching stories, and practical takeaway nuggets. As they write, 'Every decision you're making today will affect you tomorrow, so make good ones.' The best decision you can make today is to read this book."

—E.D. Hill
Mother of eight and national television and radio host

"Pat and Karyn Williams's new book, *The Takeaway*, is packed with wisdom. I'm so pleased they decided to pass it on to all of us. I loved the book and you will, too."

—George Foreman
Two-time heavyweight champion

"As a father of four girls and grandfather of ten more, I greatly identify with Pat Williams and his approach to fatherhood. And nothing can please me more than having a daughter like Karyn to echo and endorse my efforts of fathering. Life is a 'learn as you go' proposition for all of us, and nobody gets it all right. But it's so heartwarming to know that those you love return your love, and appreciate the efforts you've made on their behalf. Pat Williams is a fortunate man."

—Pat Boone
Pop music singing legend

"*The Takeaway* is a treasure chest filled with invaluable life lessons Karyn Williams has learned from her dad. These life lessons are for parents who are shaping their children's lives by what they teach them and for anyone who dares to live life in a big way! You'll be amazed at the gems you will take aw

Bestselling author

Jackson
Jackson

D1366806

"As a father of four wonderful children, I was deeply moved by the sentiments shared in *The Takeaway* by Pat Williams and his daughter, Karyn. I believe this book could radically alter the relationships of parents and their children for the better. We desperately need this in our world today. Please read this book . . . for your family's sake!"

—Jonathan Falwell
Pastor, Thomas Road Baptist Church, Lynchburg, Virginia

"Reading these endearing stories is like looking at another family's portrait and being surprised to find yourself in it! Thank you, Pat and Karyn, for sharing your lives in a way that we can all enjoy and improve our own."

—Dr. Joel C. Hunter
Senior Pastor, Northland—A Church Distributed, Longwood, Florida

"*The Takeaway* touched me both as a mother and a daughter. Not only was my heart filled with gratitude toward my own father, but as I read Karyn's musings I was reminded of the great importance of boundaries, tough love, and most important, grace, for the journey in raising my own little girl. Hats off to Karyn for such an inspiring read!"

—Shelley Breen
Point of Grace

"I really enjoyed reading the lessons Karyn learned from her dad, Pat. I see many parallels in my relationship with my own darling dad. This book is mandatory reading for every father and his daughters—sons, too!"

—Gretchen Carlson
Anchor, *FOX & Friends*

The
Takeaway

20 Unforgettable Lessons Every Father
Should Pass On to His Child

Pat Williams and Karyn Williams

with Peggy Matthews Rose

Health Communications, Inc.
Deerfield Beach, Florida

www.hcibooks.com

Library of Congress Cataloging-in-Publication Data
is available through the Library of Congress.

© 2009 Pat Williams and Karyn Williams

ISBN-13: 978-0-7573-1389-9
ISBN-10: 0-7573-1389-2

Publisher: Health Communications, Inc.
        3201 S.W. 15th Street
        Deerfield Beach, FL 33442–8190

Cover design by Kristen Vasgaard
Cover photo © iStockphoto
Interior tag photo © Karin Lau, Fotolia.com
Interior design and formatting by Lawna Patterson Oldfield

CONTENTS

Acknowledgments..ix

Introduction: The Card xiii

CHAPTER 1: Wear Your Seat Belt..............................1

CHAPTER 2: Enjoy Your Life 11

CHAPTER 3: Be Good to People 21

CHAPTER 4: There Are No Days Off....................31

CHAPTER 5: Take Care of Your Body..................47

CHAPTER 6: Exercise Your Mind.........................57

CHAPTER 7: Dare to Live Big.............................67

CHAPTER 8: Life Is About "Collecting People" 77

CHAPTER 9: There Are No Giants Out There.................89

CHAPTER 10: The World Will Take Care of the Jerks.......99

CHAPTER 11: Make Good Decisions...................113

CHAPTER 12: Are You a Leader or a Follower? 129

CHAPTER 13: You're Always Building Your Résumé........145

CHAPTER 14: Don't Spend Any Money Until
             You're Thirty..............................155

CHAPTER 15: Choose Your Friends Carefully—
             Who You Hang with Is Who
             You'll Become 167

CHAPTER 16: This Is How We Practice Not Quitting.....181

CHAPTER 17: There Are No Guarantees That You'll
             Get Along with Your Family.......................191

CHAPTER 18: Does He/She Make You a
             Better Person?............................205

CHAPTER 19: Be the Woman or Man YOU
             Want To Be 219

CHAPTER 20: Stay Close to the Lord 229

A Final Thought from Karen...........................241

About the Authors 243

To daddies and daughters everywhere,
as well as mothers and sons . . .
with the firm conviction that there is something
memorable to take away from every day
you spend together.

With love,
Pat and Karyn Williams

ACKNOWLEDGMENTS

With deep appreciation I acknowledge the support and guidance of the following people who helped make this book possible:

Special thanks to Alex Martins, Bob Vander Weide, and Rich DeVos of the Orlando Magic.

I have been highly honored to collaborate with my daughter Karyn on this book. I am very proud of her and extremely impressed with her writing ability.

Thanks also to our writing partner Peggy Matthews Rose for her superb contributions in shaping this manuscript.

Hats off to four dependable associates—my assistant Latria Leak, my trusted and valuable colleague Andrew Herdliska, my ace typist Fran Thomas, and my longtime adviser Ken Hussar.

Hearty thanks also go to my friend Peter Vegso and his fine team at HCI. Thank you all for believing that we had something important to share and for providing the support and the forum to say it.

And finally, special thanks and appreciation go to my wonderful and supportive family. They are truly the backbone of my life.

—Pat Williams

Peter Vegso, it was sitting in the car in December of 2007 that this book got its legs, and I am forever indebted to you. I will never forget your reaction to my song "Taking You with Me" when you said, "Every father in America needs to hear this." I couldn't agree more and I thank you for giving me the platform to make that happen.

To the incredible team at HCI, thank you for your unwavering belief in this project, and for faithfully seeing it through to completion.

To our writer extraordinaire, Peggy Matthews Rose. You have blown me away with your ability to turn words into the most beautiful pictures. Your sweet, gentle spirit has made working on this book such a joy.

Sincere thanks to two special friends, Kristen Vasgaard and Curt Harding. Thank you for sharing in our excitement and joining the effort to make this book the best it could possibly be.

I would like to thank Tim Fink and SESAC for welcoming me into your "family" and helping me kick-start my career in Nashville. It's going to be a fun ride!

To Dale Matthews, Stacey Wilbur, and the Brentwood Benson Publishing team. Thank you for opening the door to opportunities I once only dreamed of.

To the greatest family in the world—thank you for loving me the way you do. There is, and always will be, a little bit of all of you in me.

To the man who has brought out the woman I have always wanted to be, Brian White. You boldly believed in me from the start and have cheered me on tirelessly. Thank you for taking my dreams and giving them wings.

And finally, to my one-of-a kind dad—I am honored to call myself your daughter. God knew we'd be quite the duo when he put us together, and working on this book with you has been the greatest thrill of my life. Thank you for investing so much energy into teaching me these important life lessons. Because of you I've grown into the woman that I am.

—*Karyn Williams*

Introduction: The Card

THE MOST IMPORTANT LIFE LESSONS I LEARNED
ARE ONES THAT MY FATHER NEVER ACTIVELY TRIED TO
TEACH ME. HE SIMPLY LIVED THEM.

—Ross Hirschmann

BE NOT AFRAID OF LIFE.
BELIEVE THAT LIFE IS WORTH LIVING, AND YOUR
BELIEF WILL HELP CREATE THE FACT.

—Henry James

WHATEVER WE ACHIEVE AND WHOEVER WE ARE,
WE STAND ON THEIR SHOULDERS.

—Tim Russert, writing about fathers in Big Russ and Me

On a warm July evening in 2007, my dad, Orlando Magic executive Pat Williams, and I sat sharing a bittersweet dinner at Orlando's McCormick & Schmick's restaurant—but it wasn't the excellent seafood that made the moment memorable. It was the fact that my car was

packed to the brim, and the next morning I'd be heading to
Nashville, Tennessee. The time had come to pursue my dream
in earnest—the dream of a career in country and gospel music.

Knowing the time was drawing close to leave my family and
the community I'd grown up in, I'd spent the past few months
reflecting on life with my amazing dad. His whole life has been
about investing in others, and most of all in his nineteen (yes,
I said nineteen) kids. So one day I sat down and compiled my
personal list of all the things I have learned from my dad over
the years. Like the saying we'd heard so many times we could
recite it with him: "Wear your seat belt! Enjoy your life! Be
good to people!" Eventually it dawned on me, "That's pretty
much all you need to know in life." I don't know what com-
pelled me to write the list that day, but from the minute I began
writing, I knew deep in my heart that God had something special planned for all that distilled wisdom. Have you ever done
that—written something you knew was special, but you didn't
know just why or what to do with it? I made my list and set it
aside, trusting the moment would reveal itself in time.

Moving day approached and I racked my brain for a perfect
"going away" present for my dad. Nothing really seemed suffi-
cient. Then I remembered that list I had written months earlier.
What could be more perfect? I bought a thank-you card that was
blank on the inside, sat down, and tearfully wrote out the card.

That night in the restaurant, I handed Dad my card. As soon
as he opened it and began to read, I saw that familiar sting in

the corners of his eyes, an almost visible lump rising in his chest. "Daddy," I'd begun, and that was really all it took to pry open the floodgates. In the note, I thanked him for everything he had poured into my life and then listed the key lessons I would take away and carry for the rest of my life. "I've always been so proud to be your daughter," I ended. "Now it's time for me to go and make *you* proud!"

By the time he had finished reading, the restaurant staff was bringing out buckets and mops to wipe up all the tears. I'm not a parent yet, but I can imagine what he must have been feeling and thinking in that moment. *All those years of teaching, prompting, pushing, pulling, and nonstop cheerleading were finally paying off!* He had to be thinking, *YES! She got it! She really got it!* The proof was right there in his hands.

We sat in silence for a while, drinking in our last moments together. Then I heard my dad shout, "Karyn—this is a book!"

I'd only meant to give him a card—not write a book! But when Dad said that, I realized the special purpose for which I had made that list—so that you, young reader, can reap the same rewards I have been given, and so that you, Mom or Dad, can realize that even if you don't see it now, your kids really *are* learning from your words and your example. When they finally leave the nest to fly on their own, you'll be amazed and blessed to discover all they've taken away from life with you.

When we're young, we tend to think we have all the answers and our parents don't know anything. But what you will read on the following pages is one daughter's realization that maybe Dad *has* known what he was talking about all along. I've packed a lot of life into these thirty years so far. I have seen both incredible joy and unspeakable pain, waves of triumph and seasons of drought. Through it all, my dad has stood beside me, gently guiding my growing life. He has walked with me, holding my hand every step of the way, and carried me during the times I've lost my footing. He has poured everything he has into me, and I'm grateful for this opportunity to "pay it forward" and pass on the important lessons that have shaped me into the woman I am today.

Dad would be the first to tell you these lessons, beginning with those first three gems mentioned a few paragraphs ago, did not necessarily originate with him. But they have stood the test of time for so long, they are literally indestructible. No matter what side of the family equation you are currently on, whether you're a parent or a "child," there is something for everyone to "take away" in these lessons for all time.

Chapter 1

Wear Your Seat Belt

I T WAS JULY 28, 1995, and the morning of my sixteenth birthday. I was the first person in line at the Orlando Driver's License Bureau. As one of the last in my grade to reach that magical age, I was itching to get behind the wheel by myself. *Once I've got that license*, I thought, *look out, Orlando, here I come!*

I'd studied so hard to learn the rules of the road, but when that actual test was in front of me, why did they have to ask *those* questions? But somehow I managed them and made it outside to the actual driving test. Sitting there with an adult who wasn't my dad made me pretty nervous, but eventually I passed the test and got my license.

I couldn't believe it when my parents bought me a car. I was on top of the world! With so many siblings (there are nineteen of us and yes, you read that correctly—nineteen), in no time I became chauffeur to my younger brothers and sisters. Not quite the glamour gigs I had in mind, but at least I was the one at the wheel. I felt so grown-up and ready for anything.

As we left the house, we would always hear Dad shout, "Wear your seat belt—it's a death trap out there!" "Okaaaay, Dad," we'd groan. I thought I was so grown-up, but I was only sixteen, after all. How was I to know then that Dad was right? What I love to do more than anything in the world is sing, so with my brand-new license, I gladly accepted an invitation to sing at a church in Jacksonville, Florida. It was my first big road trip by myself. *Here I am, world!* I made the two-hour drive from Orlando to Jacksonville in one piece, sang at the church service, and the weekend was a success—a piece of cake! I floated on home.

I was driving down I-95 that Sunday afternoon, listening to the Judds sing their perfect harmonies, when a car cut over into my lane unexpectedly and the driver hit the brakes. I didn't know what to do. With adrenaline now rushing through my system, I instinctively slammed on my brakes, too, and jerked the wheel to avoid hitting the car. My brakes locked up. Before I knew it, I'd lost control of the car. My heart was in my throat as I felt the car begin spinning and spinning in circles. *This is it!* I thought. *Get ready to meet the Lord!* I kept waiting for the impact. Then the spinning stopped and the car was on its side, sliding. *Any moment now! Be merciful, Lord!* It's amazing how long a few seconds can seem when you think they are your last.

At long last the car stopped—upside down in a ditch on the side of the road. Three thoughts flashed through my mind in rapid succession:

1. *I'm still here! I'm alive!* Astonished, I drew in slow, deep breaths to be sure.
2. *Get out of the car—now!* Still breathing.
3. Dad's gonna *kill me!*

My heart was pounding, but otherwise I was okay. Eventually, I fumbled at the seat belt latch, unbuckled it, and crawled across the roof to get out of the car. Amazingly, I walked away with nothing but scrapes on my hands and knees, most of which occurred getting out of the car. I wouldn't have won any beauty contests that night, but for the moment I was so grateful to be alive, and so glad I'd had that seat belt on.

You're naked without a seat belt!

If you've ever been in an accident, you know that the days and weeks that follow are not fun. There are the calls to the insurance company, miles of forms to fill out, and the emotional trauma that always lingers, jarring you from your sleep at night and occupying most of your waking hours as well. Where do you go to find normal again?

I worried about what Dad was thinking. After all, he had *just* bought me that car. The accident occurred two months to the day since I had gotten my driver's license, and it didn't take long to find out my car was completely totaled. But physically, I was fine. "Karyn, that's all I care about," Dad said. "Cars can be replaced. I just want my little girl safe." I couldn't help feeling guilty about the accident, but in time I believed him. And I don't groan anymore when Dad says, "Wear your seat belt!" In fact, I'm the drippy faucet begging everyone to wear their seat belts! If I didn't have his voice in my head every time I got into a car, if I hadn't been belted in on that day, there is no way I'd have walked away from that accident unharmed.

So many people—especially young people who think they're invincible—act like they're "too cool" to wear a seat belt. Trust me, when your car is flying through the air or screeching across the highway, you do not have the power to save yourself. If you think you do, you're likely to be dead wrong! Or you're only going a few miles down the road and you think, *What could possibly happen?* Do you really want to find out? Seat belts were invented for a reason. It only takes a split second for an accident to happen. If you don't take the time to click your seat belt in advance, it will be too late when that second splits in front of your startled eyes.

Think of it this way: if you're sitting in a moving car without a seat belt, you should feel as naked as if you weren't wearing clothes. Highways are death traps. Have you ever noticed that most of us are doing other things while driving? No matter how many laws we pass, the roads will always be full of distracted drivers. We're talking on our cell phones, text messaging, reading, eating, or putting on makeup. I'm appalled at recent trends to put DVD players right up front—so the *driver* can see it, too! What are those manufacturers thinking? When we're driving, more than any other time, we need to focus. We don't need more distractions.

Most of what you'll read in the following chapters is about how my dad has taught me to take risks, to go for it, and not let anything stop me from putting myself "out there," becoming and remaining a viable force in my generation. While *life* may be about taking risks to succeed, driving is most certainly *not*. Don't be foolish! Don't jeopardize your life or the lives of others. If you care about your family at all, if you care about yourself (and you know you do; after all, who's the first person you look at in the mirror every morning?), please, please, *please* buckle up! If you need a little help remembering, just picture my car upside down in a ditch.

Pat's Lesson

I'll never forget the night Karyn arrived back at our house after a car accident that could have taken her life. We had spent the day at a new Disney water park that had been rented out for the Magic employees and their families. Karyn had been unable to reach any of us from the hospital where she'd been taken after the accident, so she called a friend to come pick her up. I happened to be standing on the front steps of our house when they pulled up, with no idea what had happened. She got out of the car, walked over, and buried her head in my chest, sobbing uncontrollably. Somehow, she managed to get it all out. I cried, too, as I held her, and silently prayed, "Lord, thank you for sparing my daughter."

In the 1950 classic film *All About Eve*, Bette Davis uttered the famous line, "Fasten your seat belts. It's going to be a bumpy ride." Today, those words have literally become a public service announcement—and I'm thankful. The way I see it, safety is Job No. 1, and I've made it Rule No. 1 in the Williams household for years.

It may sound like a commercial, but as my kids will tell you, I always gave them instructions in this order: "Wear your seat belt, enjoy your life, and be good to people." (My latest one is, "Do you have your sunscreen on?" There's an epidemic of skin cancer, particularly in the Sunbelt, so be forewarned and keep an SPF-30 or higher close at hand.)

I fully believe that the best way to protect our children is through teaching good habits when they're young. When they learn to respect the rules and play by them, everyone wins.

Safety may not always be fashionable ("Seat belts wrinkle my clothes!" you may protest. Yes, they do). But fashions change, and lives once damaged by the failure to play it safe cannot always be so easily repaired or altered. I recently read about a study conducted at James Madison University that revealed these startling statistics concerning seat belts:

- Approximately 35,000 people die in motor vehicle crashes each year. About 50 percent (17,000) of these people could be saved if they wore their safety belts.
- More than 90 percent of all motorists believe safety belts are a good idea, but less than 14 percent actually use them.
- Of every 100 children who die in motor vehicle crashes, at least 80 would survive if they were properly secured in an approved child safety seat or safety belts.

These facts are both heartbreaking and stunning—because they are all preventable.

Now I can't be everyone's dad—heaven knows I've tried! But I can give all of you the same advice I've given Karyn and the rest of my kids for more than thirty years now. Wear your seat belts, for goodness' sake! As the late American humorist Evan Esar once said, "It takes hundreds of nuts to hold a car together, but it takes only one of them to scatter it all over the highway." Don't let yourself or anyone you love be victimized by that one nut.

What's the number one reason for playing it safe? When you do, you're sending a message to others that you care about them, too. If an accident happens, you're telling the world it won't be on your watch if you can help it. Author Rick Warren tells us that people don't care how much you know until they know how much you care. Living safe is one of the best ways I know to tell others you care very much.

The roads on which we travel through this life are fraught with danger, but why invite trouble? Problems seem to find us easily enough without any outside assistance. Have you noticed that? There's no need at all to go looking for it.

For those who might be thinking that rules are meant to be broken, I urge you to ponder long and hard about which rules should be considered breakable. Fastening your seat belt and living your life according to the highest possible standards of safety are not rules to mess around with. They are simply not optional.

THE TAKEAWAY

"Buckle up" is a phrase we hear a lot, but please don't let it become a cliché. Listen to someone whose life was literally almost taken in an instant and to a dad who came so close to having his heart permanently broken. Don't put yourself or others through this kind of pain unnecessarily.

Wear your seat belt!

Enjoy Your Life

AS THE DAUGHTER OF A sports executive, I have lived quite an exciting life going on trips to numerous athletic events—NBA All-Star weekends, awards ceremonies, Red Sox and Phillies games. I lost count years ago. Dad never knew this, but deep down I was always a little envious of the excitement I saw in him every time we entered a new stadium or ran into an old friend of his. I never quite understood where that exhilaration came from, but I knew I wanted it in my life, too—if I could just figure out where to find it.

Dad is also a marathon runner, and in April 2005, I decided to join him. We ran our first Boston Marathon together. Of course, we *had* to go to Fenway Park and take in a Red Sox game while we were there. Dad was like a big kid. He couldn't *wait* to get to the ballpark and share with me all the energy that electric city generates on game day. As we headed down Yawkey Way just outside the stadium, Dad was practically skipping. He guided me over to the peanut stand for our all-American baseball snack. We picked up our tickets, took a quick stroll through the stadium offices to greet old friends, and then sat down (with Dad on the edge of his seat, of course) for the first pitch. I don't know who was having more fun—Dad doing what he so loved or me getting a total kick out of watching him.

Two years later, we ran the Chicago Marathon together. We were heading toward mile seven or eight when I realized Dad was singing the old Frank Sinatra song, "My kind of town, Chicago is my kind of town," under his breath. I shook my head and chuckled. Here we were, beating our bodies up in another marathon, and Dad was just singing away, having a great time. His spirit is just plain infectious.

One day a few years ago, my youngest brother, Michael, and I were commiserating over our shared struggles with figuring out where we wanted to go in life. Ever been there? So many options, but which one was "it"? How was it, we wondered, that Dad managed to be enjoying his life and his work so much after all these years?

It took me a while to see the obvious, but it finally dawned on me that the answer isn't complicated at all. Dad doesn't spend time doing things he doesn't enjoy. The world of sports is Dad's passion, and a long time ago, he made a decision to make a career out of it. I'm happiest when I'm singing, writing, listening to, or recording music. I'm a student of the music industry. I can't get enough. So the obvious decision was to get involved in what I love and figure out a way to make a living in music.

But contrary to what most singers strive for, stardom is not my end goal—it's not what really matters most to me. What counts is that I can wake up every day and *look forward* to how I will go spend the next eight hours of my life. As Dad recently reminded me, "Do things because you enjoy them, Karyn. Don't think that everything always has to lead to somewhere." That's not always an easy message to hear, but it is the truth! Any other motive for what you do ultimately leads to disappointment. But when you're doing what you love, you'll find it's hard to stop.

I've never seen anyone work as diligently and nonstop as my dad. It took me a while to figure it out, but once I'd finally immersed myself in the music industry, I discovered that secret I'd been looking for, the key to Dad's exuberance. Funny thing is, he told us what it was all the time. For as long as I can remember, I've heard Dad say, "Decide what you love to do more than *anything* in the world, and then figure out a way to get paid for it—and you'll never work a day in your life."

Do what you love!

It was really no secret at all. I just had to grow up to understand it. I don't know where you are on your life's timeline, but I hope you both hear and remember this message: *When you're doing something you're truly passionate about, it's not work.*

Oh sure, you still have to get up early and put in long hours. You're not going to love every single day on the job. Money gets tight, and life can be stressful at times. It's possible you'll get frustrated with your boss or coworkers or situations now and then. You might even need to stay late occasionally, or travel, or put off other things you'd like to do. But if you love what you're doing, that love lights up your face and makes any related pain seem so worth it. It's all just part of the struggle toward excellence, after all.

Sadly, it's way too easy to get in a rut doing what we've always done, failing to explore new frontiers or possibilities. But what's that Tony Robbins quote? "If you always do what you've always done, you'll always get what you've always gotten."

So I offer you the gift of my dad's advice—do the things you enjoy doing most. Find a way to make a living doing them if you can. If you can't, find a way to do them anyhow. Why spend every Sunday dreading work on Monday? You'll just be going through the motions of life, wondering where the joy went. Don't fret about finding that yellow brick road; just enjoy the path you are on. There doesn't have to be a wizard or a pot of gold on the other side. Perhaps you've heard the phrase, "It's not about the destination; it's about the journey." It's true! Please learn to enjoy the journey. Don't miss all there is to see along the way.

Decide what you love to do more than anything in the world, and then figure out a way to get paid for it—and you'll never work a day in your life.

Every day, we each wake up with a new chunk of time available to us. The same twenty-four hours are allotted to everyone, seven days a week. Think of it as a full bank account of time God has given you every day. You wouldn't let other people spend your money, would you? Of course not! So take back control of your time, and don't let other people spend your time by doing things you don't enjoy. It might mean finding a new job—but how bad could that be? Or it might mean taking on a new attitude in the job you currently have.

I have heard this simple but powerful piece of advice from my dad just about every day for thirty years: *Enjoy your life!* I'm grateful to have witnessed a real-life example lived out in front of me every day, too. Dad probably has no idea what a powerful example he set for us all these years. Here's a man who has worked hard and made it to the top of his field, yet in it all he remains funny, often silly, and always sentimental. He's a man who enjoys every second of the only life he's been given, and he has taught me to do likewise. Thanks, Dad—I'm truly having the time of my life. I encourage you to do whatever it takes to enjoy your life, too.

Pat's Lesson

What's my secret to enjoying life? It's simple. Spend your time doing what you love! I read not long ago about a study that has concluded happy people live longer—did you know that? So by all means, seek to be happy.

Here's what my kids have heard probably a minimum of once a day since the crib: Decide what it is you love to do the *most*, then figure out a way to get paid for it—and you'll never work a day in your life. Nothing makes me happier than a phone call from Karyn giddy with excitement over the latest song she's written or project she's been asked to be a part of. I rejoice at the thrill in her voice, knowing she is immersed in a world she loves.

I believe God wants us to enjoy the life he has given us. He put inside each of us a passion for something special—some gift or avocation through which we can make a difference. When we discover what that something special is—that thing that makes our hearts skip a beat—we'll have found our purpose, our reason for being here.

There is no doubt about it—life is hard! But it doesn't have to be a grind. The secret is finding balance and learning to enjoy the gift of life you've been given. We find that balance by steadfastly pursuing what we do enjoy.

"But Pat, I have a job! And I need that job. But there are

many aspects of that job I can't stand! Mondays depress me, and I find myself living for Friday. What do I do about that?"

Okay, that's fair. And it happens to us all at some time or another. So try this: if you hate going to your job every day, begin working toward figuring out an alternative—either a new job or a new attitude toward your old one. One of the best ways to find pleasure in your life is to spend it doing what you love, surrounded by people you love. We all need a job—but there's no reason we can't work in a field we are passionate about. The trick is to identify that one thing that makes your heart pound with excitement—and then follow it.

American inventor Thomas Edison was a hardworking man. His wife noticed it and offered him an opportunity to take a trip—to anywhere in the world he would like to go, she said. "Then I choose my laboratory," Edison answered. Edison loved his work. He was passionate about it. To him, work was not work at all.

You know you need to stay in shape, right? Well, if you hate running, find some other form of exercise you don't hate. Start walking regularly, ride a bike, use a Stairmaster at the gym, go swimming, rotate different forms of exercises so you don't get bored. You can do it. "Move it or lose it" may be an old saying, but it is true. Your body was made to move. If you stop moving, one day you may wake up to discover you no longer have a choice.

One night I sat in a church service and watched as the musicians set up for a worship concert they were about to do. Someone next to me said, "They all seem to be having such a good time." I looked over at the bebopping, bouncing man who'd been leading the worship at that church for years and realized he was a key reason behind the enjoyment the others were experiencing. It all comes down from the leadership. So if you're a leader, it is especially critical that you enjoy what you're doing. Your team is watching, and they take their cues from you.

The bottom line is this, and you're going to hear it from me over and over, just like my kids did: *It is up to you to take control of your life and start doing things you enjoy. Don't waste your time on things you don't enjoy!*

THE TAKEAWAY

We're not promised tomorrow—all we've got is today. Life is short—and time flies.

Decide what you love to do more than anything in the world, and then figure out a way to get paid for it—and you'll never work a day in your life!

Enjoy your life!

CHAPTER 3

Be Good to People

On Magic game nights over the years, I've made it a project to study my dad as he makes his way through Orlando's Amway Arena. He's always been one of the most powerful men in that building—but you never would have known it by the way he carries himself. He treats everybody the same, always has. Now, I know you've heard that before about other famous people. But think about it for a minute—it might just be one of the reasons they made it to the top of their field. Oh, no doubt they worked hard to get where they are, but successful men and women understand that just because they have CEO in front of their name or an M.D. after it, they're no different from the elevator attendant, the ticket taker, or the secretary. They treat everyone the same. Because of his example, I grew up not realizing at first that Dad was a major player in the sports world. He just does his job. He's not concerned with whether or not you know who he is.

As I mentioned earlier, the first three chapters of this book come from a phrase my dad uses every time we leave each other or hang up the phone. If he was a broadcaster, you'd call it his sign-off, he says it that regularly: "Karyn, wear your seat belt, enjoy your life, and be good to people." I smile every time I hear it, but one day it clicked for me and I thought, "Hmm . . . that pretty much sums up everything you need to know in life!" Yes, in many ways the daily grind is much more complicated than that—but in some ways it's really not.

My dad has a way of saying things that drive home the point he's making. We're all familiar with advice like, "Be kind to others" or "Treat your neighbor as yourself." But Dad's way of saying this same thing is so simple, it's absolutely profound, and it ranks among my all-time favorite "Dad advice." *Be good to people,* he says. Such a simple statement, and it sounds easy enough. But why is it so hard to do?

Nothing irritates me more than being in a restaurant and seeing a customer hassling a server over something miniscule, or being at the airport and seeing a traveler giving the woman behind the ticket counter a hard time. Why is it we often end up picking on the wrong person, snapping our mouths impatiently, and acting as though the world is here to serve us?

Try this exercise: next time you sit down at a restaurant and your server comes over, determine to look up and genuinely ask, "How are *you* today?" I've seen people in service jobs tear up over being asked that simple question, thinking, *Somebody cares!* Every time I sit down with Dad at a restaurant, I jokingly apologize in advance to the server for the interview that's about to take place. They're confused at first, but they get what I mean soon enough. First, Dad asks their name and how they're doing. They answer and usually try to move quickly to our drink order. But what they don't know is that Dad's just getting warmed up. He starts in with the questions. "Where are you originally from?" "Where did you go to college?" "What did you major in?" "Why did you choose to major in that?" "What fascinates you about that field?" "When did you graduate?" And on and on the questions go until he comes to his famous last words, "If you could be doing anything you want with your life, what would it be?" By this point, I've buried my head safely in my arms, or sometimes I've crawled under the table, where I wait until he's finished. Dad wants to know every single thing about our server. Now here's the amazing part—the transformation that takes place on their faces as this complete stranger takes a few minutes to find out a little bit about them. In mere moments they've been moved from on-the-job apathy to sheer joy.

One of my favorite things to do when I'm calling my cable or phone company is to repeat the person's name when they answer and then ask personally how they're doing. "Hey Steve, how are you today?" It catches them off guard *every time*. They're armed and ready for your complaint, certainly not expecting you to be nice. I was eating lunch with a friend of mine one day, and as our waitress laid our food down, my friend said to her, "We're going to bless our food. Is there anything

that we can pray for in *your* life?" The waitress was so taken
aback she just stood there—stunned.

When I was with Dad in Chicago one weekend, our hotel somehow confused our room
reservation with someone else's—and we
ended up in the wrong room. We were
sound asleep when the rattle of a key in the
door jarred us awake. Needless to say, my
heart jumped out of my skin. Who was break-
ing into our room? In walked a man in a business suit, pulling
a rolling suitcase, just as surprised to see us as we were to see
him. The tired traveler exploded into a rampage, screaming and
cursing loudly at my dad, demanding to know why we were in
his room. But we were just as confused as he was. I'll never forget how Dad responded. He stayed calm and apologized pro-
fusely while we gathered our things and went down to the
lobby—where we waited nearly two hours in our pajamas for
them to find another room for us.

Here's the most amazing part—Dad was running a marathon
the next day. He was exhausted and needed every bit of sleep he
could get to be rested and ready for the big event. He had every
right to be irritated, but he stayed calm and politely thanked the
hotel staff for their help as they finally led us to another room. He
could have made a scene—after all, the hotel had made the mistake. But he didn't. Instead, he chose to treat everyone involved
with respect. And I got a firsthand lesson in life management.

Treat everyone with respect!

We've all heard the phrase "don't burn your bridges," to which I would add, "You never know when you'll have to walk back across them." One of my favorite examples is of a successful Nashville songwriter. After six years of success with one publishing company, multiple number one hits and awards, he was let go from his publishing deal when the company came under new management. Unaware of his track record, the new publishers wanted to start their roster fresh with new writers. It was a major blow, both to his finances and his ego, but he held his head high, quietly packed up, and left. Obviously, the situation was completely unfair, but no matter what he was feeling, he never let a bitter word spill out of his mouth. Ten years went by, and he had a publishing deal with a different company when they were bought out by— you guessed it—the company that had let him go years before. The management involved with his release was still in place. This time, they all became friends and eventually got a big chuckle out of it. This writer understood the importance of being good to people no matter what. He could have walked out with "guns blazing" and ruined his reputation. But he understood what the Bible means when it says we should be "quick to listen, slow to speak, and slow to anger" (James 1:19). He had wisely

Don't burn your bridges . . . you never know when you'll have to walk back across them.

decided to keep his mouth shut, and ten years later the relationships came back around.

Gandhi once challenged us to, "Be the change you want to see in the world." There are small risks and great rewards available when we simply choose to be good to others. I am grateful my dad taught me this lesson every day as I was growing up in his home. I pray I will always be a woman who is kind to others and treats people with the respect, dignity, and honor they deserve.

We all have different skills and talents. I've heard it said that each of us is meant to play a role within our generation, and that if we fail to find our purpose, the world will miss out on what we had to offer. Think about what would happen—how the world would change—if everything we did was motivated by love for others rather than "me first." I think we'd see a real change.

Maybe you didn't have parents like mine who set an example for you. You can still learn it! It is never too late to begin living life the right way and to begin treating others with kindness and respect. Just think about how you would like to be treated and treat others accordingly. It really *is* as simple as that. Even in a world where the headlines might make it seem that we've turned upside down morally, I believe deep down inside we all know the right thing to do. Call it Jiminy Cricket if you want to, but listen to your conscience—and always let it be your guide. Simply treat others how you want them to treat you. It's not corny—it's common sense.

Pat's Lesson

God's plan for us is simple—he wants us to live in harmony and fellowship with each other. The basic foundation for my faith is simply this—God is love. The way I understand it, we are to love others the way he loves us. It's a reflection on him. The Gospel according to John says, "Your love for one another will prove to the world that you are my disciples" (John 13:35 [New International Version]).

I have worked hard to instill in my children the importance of this concept. The idea is that we are nice to others not because of what we can gain, but simply because it's what we are called to do. It was Henry David Thoreau who said, "Goodness is the only investment that never fails."

In a later chapter we'll discuss more fully the importance of "collecting people." But the basic concept is about developing lasting relationships that will sustain you throughout your life. One surefire way I've discovered for developing and maintaining relationships with people is to simply be good to them. There is something disarmingly attractive about treating others as you would have them treat you. It may sound surprising, but simple acts of human kindness, random or intentional, are becoming rare. Don't believe me? When was the last time you drove on America's freeways and actually observed drivers giving one another the right of way? In our garage-door opener culture, it's becoming easier every day for us to simply avoid human contact. But what way is that to live? The truth is, we're living with a dangerous loneliness, and if we're not careful, it will destroy us.

I recently heard about a high-powered CEO who declared that a secret of his success was that he "killed everyone with kindness." Not the typical big-business picture, but this man understands it's a winning formula. The good news is, kindness works for just about everyone, every time it's applied. The writer of Proverbs says it clearly, "Never let loyalty and kindness leave you! Tie them around your neck as a reminder. Write them deep within your heart. Then you will find favor with both God and people, and you will earn a good reputation" (Proverbs 3:3–4 [New Living Testament]).

When we treat people with kindness, from a business as well as a personal perspective, the obvious return on the investment is a favorable reputation. So when you're setting those short-term objectives en route to reaching your ultimate goal, make sure you put people collecting on the top of your list.

If you are a Christ follower, as I am, you know that we are called to literally be Christ to others in this world, and that means loving everyone unconditionally. God loved us when we were unlovable and claimed us when we were the outsider. Shouldn't we do the same for others? Our job here on Earth is to try and be the right person, not point out the wrongs of others or treat them in a way that is condemning. Most times, we're quick to "throw stones" and point out the wrongs of others. But God wants us to be watching each other's back.

I recently interviewed author Hal Urban for my weekly radio show. During the course of the interview, Hal told me an interesting story. He had been reading his Bible and came across 1 Corinthians 16:14, where the apostle Paul advises us to "do everything in love." Hal was about to embark on a four-day speaking tour, so he thought, *I'm going to put that verse into practice.* For four days on the road he did everything in love with every person he met— people at the airport, hotel clerks, cab drivers, everyone he came into contact with. Everywhere he went, he did everything in love. By the time he got home, he told his wife, "I've just had the four best days of my life. Putting that little verse into practice changed everything for me."

I was about to take off on a four-day trip as well when Hal told me that story, so I decided, *I'm going to do that, too.* And I discovered the same thing Hal did. I had the four best days of my life as well. So join the club—the Do Everything in Love Club. The dues are free and the rewards eternal.

THE TAKEAWAY

Let's be the change we're looking for!

It doesn't get much simpler than this piece of advice my dad gives me almost every day.

Lay down your stones, take a genuine interest in others, and simply . . .

Be good to people!

CHAPTER 4

There Are No Days Off

There is a special place in the hearts of the Williams children for a Christmastime show at Walt Disney World's Epcot Center called "Holiday Splendor." My brother Bobby and I performed in it for several years. The show starred the famous Broadway actress Carol Lawrence, and we were the two kids who sang and danced with her. To this day, when we all get together at Christmas, someone will break out a line or song from the show and we all get a good laugh.

I first tried out and got the part in 1986. Initially, my brother Bobby wanted nothing to do with it, but as soon as he saw the first show, he changed his tune. The following year, we were both selected and got to perform together. At that age, Bobby and I looked a lot alike, and there was a magical blending of our voices when we sang. People often mistook us for twins. That experience goes down in my book as the most valuable that Bobby and I have ever shared.

When the 1988 tryouts rolled around, I walked into the audition hall believing the exercise was just a formality. After all, I had proven myself for the past two years, hadn't I? Bobby and I did our usual thing with our usual panache and I walked out of the room, confident the part was mine. Then they called the names. Mine was not among them.

What had happened? Surely there must be a mistake. To make it worse, Bobby made it—and I *didn't*. What? I was the whole reason he'd wanted to try out in the first place! This was an outrage! It was wrong, that was all. Just wrong. Someone had made a mistake.

But, no. No outrage. No conspiracy. No mistake. No one was out to get me. The problem was I'd been so confident I'd get the part, I just didn't try as hard. Because of my prior involvement, my parents knew the judges personally and asked them afterward why my name hadn't been called. One of the judges said, "The sparkle that's usually in Karyn's eyes just *wasn't there* tonight."

I spent the rest of that winter in misery—but I'd learned a powerful lesson. It was simply this—you've got to "bring it" *every single time*. As Dad would say, "There are no days off!" but I'd decided to take that night "off," trusting that my track record spoke for itself. Wrong decision.

The following winter, Bobby and I were both awarded roles in the show. As usual, Carol's performances were consistently flawless. One night in between shows, we were backstage and I saw Carol limping terribly. I ran over to ask what was wrong, just as she was taking off one of her shoes. That's when I saw that two of her toes were taped together. Carol explained she had broken them a few weeks earlier. I processed what she said and realized she had been dancing "wounded" for the entire Christmas season. Her level of dedication and professionalism —to the point of performing in pain—made a real impact on my young life.

Dad will tell you that there was a time when most of us kids in the house were in our teens—at the same time. In his speeches then I often heard Dad say, "There was a time when sixteen of my children were all teenagers at the same time—that was the year I learned why some animals eat their young!" *Very funny, Dad,* I remember thinking. Then he'd go on to say, "My teenagers think they're working hard, but they're really not." At the time, we didn't appreciate his saying that. Now I know just how right he was. I thought of Dad when I recently read this quote from the late performer Ben Bergor, "It is amazing how quickly the kids learn to drive a car, yet are unable to understand the lawn mower, snowblower, or vacuum cleaner." It's true!

We had a large, beautiful home on the lake and we loved it. But Dad made it very clear to each of us that when we reached the age of eighteen, we were leaving. In true Pat Williams's fashion, he gave us three options:

1. Go to college
2. Sign up for the military
3. Enter the workforce

I even seem to remember Dad playing "The Party's Over" instead of the "Happy Birthday" tune when that day arrived! The bottom line is that by eighteen, Dad wanted us to understand we were now young adults, ready for the world and responsible for ourselves. No more staying home playing video games—that was absolutely not an option. He promised to get us through college, if we wisely chose that path, but that's when the funding ended. "No more free lunches," he would say. At eighteen, it was time for the Williams kids to go to work and make it on our own.

It's important to note that he didn't spring this news on us on our eighteenth birthdays. We knew all along that "D-Day" was coming. Mentally, he prepared us to understand what was expected of us and to be ready when that day arrived. That's an important point to keep in mind if you're a parent reading this or a person who hopes to be a parent one day. Helping your kids to be ready and to plan for their futures is far better than reaching a boiling point one day and suddenly showing them the door. I've seen that happen to more of my friends than I want to admit, and that is a road of heartbreak and pain. Save yourselves the agony and own up to your expectations early on. You and your child can only benefit from such transparency in your relationship.

Nothing frustrates me more than watching parents supporting adult children. As kids, we're good at making excuses for why we don't have enough money. But the reason is simple—

let me just go ahead and state the truth here—*they don't want to work.* Parents, I know there's a tendency to feel guilty and think, "But if I don't help them out, what will happen?" Trust me, they'll survive. Here's how I look at it—if I don't want to work, then I have two choices: (1) go live in a shelter, or (2) sleep in the backseat of my car. It's that simple. It is not my dad's responsibility to come up with *my* rent money every month! Parents, your kids know what to expect from you. They know they can come to you with their sob story about how they're trying desperately to find a job, but the economy is bad, no one is hiring, it doesn't fit in with their current schedule, and on and on and on. They know you'll feel sorry for them and bail them out—again. It's up to you to set clear boundaries and explain when the funding ends. As kids, we're constantly trying to push the envelope and see just how much and for how long we can get away with things. You may be complaining about the fact that your child can't or won't keep a job. But if they know they can come to you every few weeks for their rent money, then what incentive do they have for keeping a job?

My dad had a game he would play with us to help us mentally prepare for "life on our own." "Karyn," Dad would say, "would you rather be teaching school or delivering the five o'clock newscast?" "Doing the news," I'd respond. "Okay. Would you rather be delivering the news or

Mom and Dad are not meant to be your permanent meal ticket.

coaching gymnastics?" "Doing the news," I'd respond again. "Would you rather be doing the news or singing on Broadway?" "I'd rather be singing on Broadway." And on and on the game would go. It challenged us to picture what we wanted to do in life. It also taught us to think ahead to a time when we would have to do one of those things to support ourselves. That's a great little game you can play with your kids, and it's a non-threatening way to get them to open up about their likes and dislikes and to ultimately discover where their true passions lie.

For you younger readers, please understand that Mom and Dad are not meant to be your permanent meal ticket. Your parents' home is where you get your foundation for the life you were born to live. Just as grade school gets you ready for junior high and junior high for high school, and so on, the home you grow up in is your prep school, as it were, for living life on your own. It's the nest from which you learn to fly—and go on to build a nest of your own.

Dwight Bain, a counselor friend of ours in Orlando, says the number one counseling issue he deals with is that of adult children who won't leave home. Would you believe there are 13 million adult children in this country still living with their parents? That's the equivalent of all the people in the entire state of Florida. I know every family has to make their own decisions and that there are exceptions for every rule, but living off Mom and Dad, rent free and with the housekeeping done for you, is not a bad deal. It's also not healthy long-term.

That didn't happen in the Williams household. At eighteen we were out the door and on our own. And while it seemed a little scary at the time, I believe that's the way it should be. Now that all nineteen of us have passed that milestone, when we come home for Thanksgiving and Christmas, we have joyous occasions and enjoy being back in the fold. But no one "lives" at home full-time except the two who pay the mortgage.

In the 1996 film *Jerry McGuire*, Tom Cruise talks to Cuba Gooding Jr. in the locker room about his job in sports management. "It is an up-at-dawn, pride-swallowing siege," he said, and I laugh whenever I hear the line. But it's true. We're all looking for a ride down "easy street." But let me save you a lot of time here and tell you that *it doesn't exist!* There is no easy way. I think there's a moment in everyone's life when those ten two-letter words that drove the life of golfer Ben Hogan finally sink in: "If it is to be, it is up to me." I encourage you to let that moment come early for you. Please understand that the world doesn't "owe" you anything. The sooner it sinks in, the more time you'll have to live a happier, fuller, more successful life.

The world doesn't owe you!

I've mentioned elsewhere in this book that I was a gymnast growing up. I loved it all— sprinting down the runway and then flying off the springboard over the vault, swinging free on the uneven bars, landing a dismount off the balance beam, nailing the perfect floor routine—

my blood is pumping right now just writing about it. Oh, how I loved gymnastics! In my dreams I could see myself winning major competitions, and one day having a medal placed around my neck at the Olympics. One of my heroines during that time was Olympic gold medalist Shannon Miller. Every day, Dad would cut out articles from newspapers and magazines about Shannon. One quote of hers from that time has really stayed with me: "When you are not practicing, someone somewhere is, and when you meet her—*she will win.*" That's a pretty powerful statement and one I remind myself of often. While I never became an Olympic medal–winning gymnast and eventually realized there were other things I could do better, I've grown up understanding there's just no substitute for hard work.

When I was in elementary school, my grandmother tried to teach me how to play the piano. The emphasis here is on "tried." We sat down each week for our lesson and she would ask, "Did you practice this week?" I usually fumbled around and tried to convince her that I had, but my patient grandmother would simply start from the beginning—again. In those days I wasn't all that interested in working very hard at learning piano or any instrument. I just wanted to sing. "Why do I need to know how to play an instrument?" I wondered. The older I've gotten, the more I have regretted that decision—especially now that I've become entrenched in the Nashville community and have to bring a guitar player every time I sing out.

So recently I made a decision. I took off my acrylic nails

(girls, you *know* what a big deal that is!), called a guitar teacher recommended by a friend, set up lessons, and bought a small keyboard to keep at my house to "relearn" the piano. "Isn't it a little late in life for you to be doing all of these things?" people have asked. "Are you kidding? Not at all!" I respond. As my dad would say, it's only too late when they pull the plug on the respirator. Until then, I'm the only person who has the power to change myself.

It's never too late to go for it and learn something new. Yes, it's going to take some serious work to make up for the lost years, but I'm willing to do it. "It takes shoe leather to the pavement—every day!"—*another* of Dad's favorite sayings. Former Olympic pole-vaulter the Reverend Bob Richards, who was one of the first athletes to appear on a Wheaties box, observed, "A bowl of Wheaties every day and about 10,000 hours of hard work can take you anywhere you want to go in life." I think I've got about 9,000 hours to go and I'm still eating those Wheaties.

If you want something badly enough, you've got to invest in obtaining it. You really can't cheat, steal, or lie your way to the top of the game. You may read stories about people who attempted it and even got away with it for a while—but, eventually, lazy or dishonest ways will trip you up. Today, I am literally learning to sing for my supper. Whatever it is you do best, I can't encourage you enough to work hard to be better at it every day. Make excellence your endgame.

People wonder how my dad does it all. Professionally, he's a hugely successful sports executive, a motivational speaker who's always on the go, the author of more than fifty books, and a major player in the Orlando community. Personally, he's a husband, father to nineteen children, grandfather to seven more, a Sunday school leader at First Baptist Orlando and a mentor to many young lives. And if that's not enough, he's a voracious reader, finishing at least one book a day (with about five others in progress). I confess, I've watched him and I don't know how he does it. It could have something to do with something else I've always heard him say: "Do what has to be done. Do it when it has to be done. Do it to the best of your ability. And do it that way every time." Whatever his secret is, my dad inspires me to work hard every day at living the one and only life I've been given. As much as it is up to me, I intend to do him proud by following his example.

Here in Nashville, we have what we call "writers in the round" where writers of popular hit songs (not always the artists who sing them) sit down and sing with an acoustic guitar and share their songs. It's a very intimate setting, and very special to listen to the writer play an acoustic version of the song.

One night, I was at the legendary Bluebird Café, listening to a round with several hit songwriters—Rivers Rutherford, who wrote "Real Good Man" for Tim McGraw; Chris Wallin, who wrote "Don't Blink" for Kenny Chesney; Dave Berg, who wrote "If You're Going Through Hell" for Rodney Atkins and

"Moments" for Emerson Drive; and Liz Rose, who has written the huge Taylor Swift hits like "Teardrops on My Guitar," "Tim McGraw," and "Picture to Burn."

Liz began writing with Taylor Swift when Taylor was a fourteen-year-old unsigned artist. Liz decided to take a chance on this young girl, who at the time had nothing more than big dreams and gut-wrenching determination. Since Taylor was still in school, the only time they could schedule to write was in the late afternoons.

Now songwriters do their "thing" like any other working stiff—by sitting down and plugging away at it all day, every day. Typically, the writer will schedule no more than two appointments per day—one midmorning and one midafternoon. By the time the 5:00 PM whistle blows, they're ready to go home, just like everyone else.

That night at the Bluebird Café, Liz Rose said something that hit me like a truck and really drove home my dad's point about working hard. As she introduced the song she was about to play, she said, "I wrote this song with a girl named Taylor Swift. We had a standing appointment every Tuesday afternoon at 4:00 PM. When everyone else was heading home, I was writing my third song of the day."

Seven cuts and three million records later, I'd say her hard work paid off. Because of her willingness to work hard and put in long hours, her life has been forever changed. Her success has opened the door to cuts on Taylor's upcoming record and has elevated her name to the top of the "best" list in a very competitive industry. Many people would call Liz Rose irreplaceable.

If you want to be irreplaceable, too, determine to be a person who wakes up every day ready to write just one more song, and to fall into your bed at night exhausted, knowing that you've given it everything you've got! It's a great way to live. I should know. I've been watching my dad do it every day of my life, and now I'm living that way, too.

Pat's Lesson

In our vacation-obsessed society, we might be tempted
to look for reasons not to work. But I have to agree with
anthropologist Margaret Mead, who said, "I learned the
value of hard work from working hard."

Most of us have been miraculously blessed with able
bodies and sound minds that are made for a mission. We
are not here by accident! Nor are we given the gift of life
simply to squander it watching television or playing video
games. Believe me when I tell you that at the end of your
days, you will wonder where it all went so quickly. We've
got to make the most of what we've been given—and that
means having a willingness to work hard every day.

Yes, we need to rest occasionally, but the body was made
to work. All my life, I've been driven by a desire to accomplish something, and I've made sure my kids heard that
message. Now I want to share it with the world. We all
need a reason to get up every day! Working toward a goal
gives you that reason. "There ain't no such thing as a free
lunch" is another saying the Williams kids are likely tired
of by now. It may not be grammatically correct, but it is
true. There's no substitute for hard work.

Artist Vincent Van Gogh understood that, "Great things
are not done by impulse, but by a series of small things

brought together." If we work toward our goal a little bit each day, it's amazing what we can accomplish. I once heard a story about a man who wanted to build his own airplane. He set his mind to it and made sure that he did something every day, no matter how tired he was after work—even if it was just to turn a screw. Over time, that airplane came together, and he literally soared to new heights—all because he was faithful to the task at hand and kept after the small things.

Clothing designer Ralph Lauren said, "The key to longevity is to keep doing what you do better than anyone else. We work real hard at that. It's about getting your message out to the consumer. It's about getting their trust, but also getting them excited, again and again." There's that stick-to-it-ivity concept I love so much—a word Walt Disney coined. You've got to be good at what you do and then never give up. The horse that stays in the race is far more likely to win than the horse that wears out and gives up after the first couple of laps. And then you've got to keep yourself relevant.

So when I say there are no days off, what I mean is that we should always have the end goal in mind, every day of our lives. Yes, we can and should take time for goofing off. I think that might even be in the Bible somewhere. I'm not talking about being hard around the edges and no fun to be with, or someone whose idea of a good time is painting the town beige.

But we can and should make every day productive in some way. No less a genius than Thomas Alva Edison once opined, "The three great essentials to achieve anything worthwhile are, first, hard work; second, stick-to-itiveness; third, common sense." I've told you here what I told my kids every day of their lives: work hard every day, never give up, and use your head. I think old Tom and I would have gotten along well.

Here's a great illustration, and it's one I picked up several years ago when I spoke at an event celebrating Martin Luther King Jr.'s birthday. When there, I met a woman named Clara Walters with the Orange County (Florida) School Board who told me about growing up on a farm in Deland, Florida.

"At the end of the summer," she said, "it was time to cut the cabbages. We rode on a cart as we moved in between the rows, holding a machete in one hand to chop the cabbages. However, I held two machetes, one in each hand. I was whacking those cabbages on both sides of the cart and got twice as much done. It has carried forward throughout the rest of my life. Here at the Orange County School Board, they can never get rid of me. It would take two people to replace me because I am a cabbage cutter."

THE TAKEAWAY

Dad reminds me all the time that the two most important words in the English language are—WHAT ELSE? "What else can I offer? What else can I bring? What else can I contribute?

Just remember—Good things come to those who wait, but only what's left behind by those who hustle!!

CHAPTER 5

Take Care of Your Body

In Kenny Chesney's song "Living in Fast Forward," he says, "Our body's a temple, that's what we're told; I've treated this one like an old honky-tonk." Isn't that so true of many of us? I shudder to think of some of the things I've put this poor body of mine through! As young people, we think we're indestructible. We Generation Xers think our knees will last forever, that our hair will always be the young vibrant color it is now, and that we'll never develop wrinkles. Well, I know a baby boomer or two who admits to thinking the same things not that many years ago, and now they're lining up for glucosamine, Botox, and L'Oreal.

It's time for all of us to wake up and realize, *the decisions I'm making today really are going to affect me in the future*—good or bad. Worshipping the sun during your youth will surely haunt you down the road. From what I hear, those skin cancer treatments are no day at the beach. Smoking, eating junk food, a sedentary lifestyle, too much alcohol, lack of sleep—all of the things we do when we're young are going to affect us down the road. What is it about us that makes us think we're invincible when we're young?

In addition to his regular reminders, Dad has always set a great example when it comes to treating his body well. I was reminded of this fact when I accompanied him on a trip to Chicago back in my college days. We were late leaving our hotel, so I was hurrying us along when Dad stopped to drink down an entire bottle of water. "Come onnn, Daaad!" I moaned.

After guzzling down the last drops, he said in that silly broadcaster voice of his, "Just hang on, Kris! [One of his nicknames for me comes from my middle name, Kristyne.] I want my blood pumping freely through my veins for a long time!" It's amazing how things like that stay with you.

Guard your health!

All these years later, whenever I drink from a water bottle (which is pretty much all day every day), I have this funny vision of my blood running happily through my veins because of all the water I drink. Silly? Yes, completely! But what a testimony to how powerful *one statement* can be, even in a moment when I'm sure Dad wasn't trying to "teach" me anything. I remember hearing once that if you put a T-bone steak in a bowl of a certain soft drink, it will be gone in two days, eaten up by all the citric acid in the soda. Did you *know* that? Just imagine what that same soda is doing to the inside of your stomach! We are so much better off—not to mention having happier veins—when we reach instead for a bottle of good old H_2O.

Parents, the example you're setting in this area is subtle. It's not necessarily something you sit down and "teach" your children —it's more of a lifestyle message. If you want your kids to eat right, are you doing it yourself? Are you making sure you exercise every day and seeing the dentist regularly? If we don't take care of ourselves, we are likely to one day become a burden to others. I know it doesn't "feel" like that right now, but people I know who are forty and older tell me when you get there, you'll be surprised how fast it happened. Our health is a precious gift, and it's our responsibility to safeguard it any way we can.

Think about the story of Lance Armstrong. Ever heard of him? At twenty-two, he became the U.S. National Cycling Champion. As a professional athlete, Lance worked hard and took good care of himself. He knew it mattered if he was to excel in his field, and he did. But in the middle of all this glory, Lance Armstrong discovered an awful truth. He had cancer. At just twenty-five, he thought his career—and maybe even his life—was over. Of course, history now tells us he beat back the cancer and went on to win bicycle's coveted Tour de France seven years in a row (1999–2005) before retiring at the ancient age of thirty-seven. Now that might sound old to you right now, but it will be here before you know it. You can be sure Lance Armstrong knows he is not invincible, and he knew it when he was a young man. As this book was being written, we learned that Armstrong announced a comeback, so obviously taking care of himself has paid off.

Think of the recent news stories about people like Anna Nicole Smith and her son Daniel. Talk about gone before your time! They were both so young, but because they'd lived a hard lifestyle that definitely did not include taking good care of their bodies, the world has been robbed of their potential.

> *Our health is a precious gift, and it's our responsibility to safeguard it any way we can.*

The older I've gotten, the more I appreciate the fact that Dad has taken care of his health the way he does. It shows me that he values his family enough to want to take care of himself for us. Of course, as kids we'd always tease him about the "cardboard" cereal he would eat from the health food store, or we'd gripe about the fact that we were never allowed to order dessert at a restaurant. But now that he is sixty-nine and in perfect health, I appreciate the fact that, Lord willing, he'll be around for a long time! Dad's example has taught me that food shouldn't be looked at as an enemy. It's an important tool for our health that, if used properly, will sustain us the way God intended.

One of the things Dad loves to do is run. He's always been into doing something physical to keep his body challenged, but would you believe he started running marathons when he was in his fifties? That's not the kind of thing most people older than forty would just wake up and decide to do one day. Dad even decided to try mountain climbing in 1996—when he was fifty-six years old! I think of him as fearless, at least when it comes to trying something new. He knows that if we don't, one day our bodies just give up. So that's what he modeled for me: treat your body well and it will return the favor. Because of his example, I've become a marathon runner, too. He's not the kind of dad who will sit around and drink a beer with you—he's the kind of dad who will challenge you to keep up with *him* during a marathon! How cool is that?

Just as we were finishing this book, Dad called to say he had caught thirty-two innings at the New York Yankees fantasy camp, and eight days later he caught forty more in the Phillies fantasy camp. If my math is correct, that's three ten-inning games one weekend and four more ten-inning games the next! I don't know how my dad's knees hold up, but he was squealing on the phone like a teenager after playing ball with some of his baseball heroes.

While I've got country songs on my mind (and I always do), by now you've likely heard Tim McGraw's "Live Like You Were Dyin'." In it, Tim tells the story of a man who finds out he might be living on borrowed time. Friends, we are all on borrowed time, from the moment we are born. Please honor the body God has given you and treat it well while you can!

Pat's Lesson

Of all the lessons I've made sure the Williams family hears from me, one of the most important is that of honoring the body God gave you. It thrills me to sit down in a restaurant with Karyn and hear her order water instead of soda—and to know that she is running and exercising on her own. Far too many of us think we can get away with a steady diet of junk food. The day arrives, sooner or later, when those who live by that philosophy discover it's time to pay the piper—and the toll he exacts makes even our annual tax bill seem like Monopoly money in comparison. Bad eating habits can be costly on your health, your family, your future—and ultimately the future of those who love you.

"Take care of your body," is a message young people regularly hear from me. It's a philosophy about which I am passionate, because I know how quickly "young" stops being used as an adjective to describe us.

People ask me all the time why I work out so hard every day, why I eat some really weird-looking healthy stuff—well, the answer is very simple: I am getting in shape for old age. The more I study the life of one of my heroes, Walt Disney, I'm convinced his philosophy applies to all of us: make today pay off tomorrow. That goes for our health as well. So everything I'm doing today is an investment to pay dividends tomorrow. When I'm eighty-five years old, I want to be able to wear out my grandchildren! It's the only way I can get back at their parents for what they did to me! The truth of the matter is, I've set a goal—I want to live to be one hundred. I want Willard Scott on national television to give me a case of Smucker's jelly on my hundredth birthday. So I'm investing right now to live to be one hundred, Lord willing.

Coach John Wooden, the great UCLA coach and one of my heroes, is still speaking and writing books at ninety-eight. He's so busy, it's hard to get on Coach Wooden's calendar. That's how I want to do it! I've always stressed to my children that everything you're doing today in caring for your body—what you eat, the rest you get, staying away from tobacco, drugs, and alcohol—everything you're doing now is an investment to pay dividends in your future. The more I study about health, the more I'm convinced that the two prime ingredients—the two nonnegotiable items—are eating properly, with lots of fruit and vegetables, and a regular program of exercise.

Years ago, I remember hearing Uta Pippig, the great marathoner, say, "The body was made for action. The man sitting on the couch—he's living dangerously."

During speaking events, I often tell the apocryphal story of calling George Burns. I asked him what it would take to live to be one hundred. "Well," he said, "the first thing you've got to do is to get to be ninety-nine—and then for one year be very careful." Burns went on, "My financial advisors tell me to keep investing in futures. Futures? I don't even order green bananas anymore!" I asked him, "George, what's the greatest advantage of being a hundred?" "Very little peer pressure," he said. I'm looking forward to that time.

I once heard my friend Dodgers announcer Charlie Steiner on ESPN's SportsCenter announce that a ballplayer was injured and his condition was "day-to-day." Charlie added, "Aren't we all!"

As we were writing this book, America lost two respected broadcast journalists within a month of each other and at roughly the same age—Tim Russert and Tony Snow. I don't know about Tim's habits, but I've read that Tony took every precaution to avoid developing the cancer that had taken his mother years earlier. Yet both these men died, as we might say, "before their time." Folks, none of us really knows when our time will be up. Take care of your health while you have it. Make it your goal to live every moment of your life in peak condition, as far as it is up to you.

I really wouldn't mind having a *little* peer pressure when I get to be one hundred. I'd like to have you in that rocking chair next to me. Take care of your body, and I'll see you then!

THE TAKEAWAY

Our bodies are not indestructible.

Every decision you're making today will affect you tomorrow, so make good ones.

Show the people you love that you care enough about them to take care of yourself, for their sake as well as your own.

Take care of your body!

CHAPTER 6

Exercise Your Mind

I never quite understood my dad's obsession with books. I mean, he is absolutely *addicted* to reading! He believes in it so much, he even wrote a book about reading, believe it or not, titled *Read for Your Life* (HCI, 2007). A book is never more than a few inches away from his hands, and every time we're together, a trip into Borders or Barnes & Noble is somewhere on the agenda. Lately I've been realizing how valuable his example has been. He utilizes every second of his day to challenge himself in every way possible. Remember that old coffee ad that ended with the words, "Good to the last drop"? Well, that's my dad. He squeezes every last drop out of *every single day!*

Dad has a very addictive personality, but fortunately he has chosen to channel his "addictions" in positive ways. What a great example this has been to his children. Isn't that how we'd all like to live? If you've got to have an obsession, make it a healthy one.

Not too long ago, Dad said to me, "Karyn, you'll never be

lonely if you have a good book around." He's right! (I would argue that you'll never be lonely with a good book *and* some good music! But I'll let him have his point.) I was stunned when I read in Dad's book that reading as a pastime is on the decline. Well, maybe I wasn't completely surprised—it's clear that video games, iPods, the Internet, and all manner of electronic devices have captivated our attention. We have so many other "more exciting" options at our fingertips. Still, the news made me sad to hear. Why don't more people want to read? I think the secret is in reading things you're interested in. I recently began reading the Left Behind book series—and if you know how many books Tim LaHaye and Jerry B. Jenkins wrote in that set, you know I'll be occupied for quite some time. Now, I'm not a fast reader, but I have flown through those books so far. They are bona fide page-turners. I just can't put them down. I'm addicted! Now I see what my dad always meant when he said, "Don't ever pick up anything you're not interested in or you won't read it."

But reading, I've learned, is functional as well as entertaining. I vividly remember a time when my dad used books to lift me out of a minor "funk" I was going through. I was in my early twenties and struggling with whether or not I was fulfilling God's purpose for my life. I imagine we all want to know we're on the right path before we've gone too far down the wrong one. Since I was feeling a little "down" in general, I knew a lunch with Dad was in order. So I bent his ear for a while. I didn't feel like my real estate job was a big enough contribution to society; I wanted to be singing more gigs in Orlando; I didn't think I'd ever meet "Mr. Wonderful." You know those days when everything just feels "blah." I realize now I was having a passion problem—I just didn't care that much about anything I was doing. But at the time I couldn't quite see what was wrong.

Books are mental dental floss!

Wisely recognizing I just needed a little kick in the behind, at the end of lunch Dad threw out a challenge. I'll give you a minute to put on your surprised face here—it was a reading challenge! Dad said, "Karyn, I challenge you to read five books in the next five weeks and come back and give me reports on each of them." "What? That's one book a week," I cried. "I don't read as fast as you. And besides, I don't have the time for that!"

But Dad promised me that if I'd take his challenge, I would notice a difference in my life. Grudgingly, I decided to take him on. I went to our closest Borders to choose my five books. Remembering Dad's advice about not picking up anything I wasn't interested in, I headed for the psychology section. I've always been fascinated by human behavior and psychology, so I picked up four books on that subject. For my fifth book, I chose a Christian novel that looked interesting.

For the next five weeks, I read like crazy. I'm fiercely competitive (I am a Williams child) so I was determined to rise to

Dad's challenge. I became so immersed in these books that I found myself cutting out other things from my schedule, just so I could get home to read. At the end of the first week, I couldn't wait to call Dad and fill him in on what that first book was about.

As the weeks went on, I slowly realized what Dad had done. That day we'd had lunch, as I was toasting myself at my own pity party, my wise old dad understood what I needed most was to get my mind off "me." Books can do that in amazing ways.

The first sentence of one of the most popular books of all time, *The Purpose Driven Life* by Rick Warren (Zondervan, 2002), simply says, "It's not about you!" I love that, and how true it is. It's human nature, sadly, to get so wrapped up in our own lives that we can't see past the ends of our noses. We become oblivious to anything and anyone else. And life races past us.

Read for one hour—from a book—every day!

Later in this chapter, Dad will offer you his favorite reading challenge. I don't want to steal his thunder, but it involves reading every day. Here's my addition in advance to what Dad has to say—take the time to write every day as well. It can be anything—a letter, a poem, a song, a crossword puzzle, or even an e-mail—and I don't know if any of us can get through the day without writing at least one e-mail anymore.

Writing truly feels like a gift I've been given. It is my outlet.

I've always said, "I usually write better than I talk!" But it doesn't matter if writing is your gift or not. We can all *learn* to write. In fact, if you want to be a person who is understood, I can think of no better skill to develop than clear writing. For me, it's often a therapy session of sorts. After I've had a chance to write about something, then I can tell you what I actually think about it. There's something about letting the thoughts travel down your arms and out through your fingers that helps you understand them better.

If you think about it for a while, you'll realize books are the way we learn about what matters most to us, and they're the way we pass knowledge on to the next generation. In mentoring situations we can influence a few people, but with books that influence is unlimited. Where would we be without books—I mean, really?

I know that you and I have a long time yet before we need to really worry about things like dementia or Alzheimer's disease, but I've come to realize that exercising your mind is a lot like exercising your body. If you don't get into the habit when you're young, it just gets harder and harder to do. When we're young, everything is much more flexible—including our priorities. Let's agree to make exercising our minds on a regular basis part of our daily routine. Are you in? You won't regret it.

Pat's Lesson

As Karyn has witnessed many times over, rare is the moment you'll see me without a book in my hands. Everywhere I speak, I tell my audiences, "Books are like mental dental floss." And it's true! By now, they've figured out how to attach a machine to just about every muscle in the human body to give it a workout—except for the brain. Books are like strength training for your mind.

There is mounting evidence that regular reading helps ward off Alzheimer's—and who doesn't want to defeat that evil beast? Can your reading example make a difference for others? Absolutely—if you commit to reading every single day.

Whenever I speak, I present a reading challenge to my audiences. My challenge is simply this—read for one hour a day, from a book, every day for the rest of your life. At the end of one week, you'll have finished a regular-size book. At the end of one year, you'll have finished fifty-two books, and at the end of ten years, you'll have read 520 books. Did you know that if you read five books on any given subject, you'll be considered a world-leading authority on that subject? It's true. So at the end of one year you could be an expert on ten different subjects. In ten years, you could be a world-leading authority on one hundred different subjects if you so desire. The news media could be coming to you for interviews! Do you think that would make a difference in your life? Your earning capacity?

I'm often asked, "What should I read?" My answer is always the same: "A subject you're interested in." In fact, never pick up a book you're *not* interested in (this is after you've left school, by the way). I read in my fields of interest—baseball, Civil War history, World War II, leadership, biographies, Christian inspiration. I read what I care about.

Not long ago I took my daughter Kati out for dinner. She had a present for me, a T-shirt she'd seen somewhere. On the front of the shirt there was a picture of three books. Below the graphic were the words, "Read 'em and reap!" There's no better way to exercise that cranial muscle. It craves exercise.

I went to a Borders bookstore with a sign on the front that said "Borders Books: A 24-hour gym for your imagination." Exactly!

When I see people coming out of the movies or who've just burned up an hour or more watching television, their expressions say, "Eh, I just killed a couple of hours, but it was nothing great." Let me tell you that when you finish a good book that really stirs your mind up, you'll never say, "It was all right." If it was only "all right," you'd likely have put it down before you finished the first chapter! No, after you've read a book, every part of your body is alive.

If you need further evidence that reading is the best choice for filling up your leisure time, consider this: when you read a book you are using primarily natural energy— the kind you've been given by God and that's available to you every day. What better way can you think of to "go green"?

THE TAKEAWAY

In my planner, I carry a card my dad wrote to me on my twenty-fourth birthday that includes six pieces of "fatherly advice." Number 2 is this:

"Be a lifelong learner. To the person who graduates and stops learning tomorrow, he'll be uneducated the day after."

Exercise your mind!

CHAPTER 7

Dare to Live Big

Dare to Live

THERE'S A BIG OLD WORLD OUTSIDE MY DOOR.
AIN'T GONNA SIT AND WATCH IT SPIN BY NO MORE,
'CAUSE IT AIN'T SLOWING DOWN OR WAITING ON ME.
I'M GONNA GRAB WHAT I CAN WHILE IT'S WITHIN MY REACH.

—*Williams/White/Dean*

In college, I entered the Miss University of Florida contest, just on a whim really. No one was more surprised than I was when I won. That victory put me in competition for Miss Florida, and while I didn't win the top prize, I did come in as first runner-up. Not only that, but I won the talent and interview portions of the competition against fifty other young Florida women. I'll tell you more about that experience in Chapter 12, but something in that little triumph helped me see I could reach higher and farther if I just tried. It also helped me realize that singing was my true passion. I love music—bet you hadn't guessed that, had you?

So when I was presented with a singing opportunity shortly after the competition, I decided to take a semester off from school to pursue it. Bad choice. Before I knew it, the opportunity turned to dust and the semester had turned into three years. The more time that went by, the more hopeless I felt about ever getting my degree. The rosy glow of that beauty contest victory had long ago morphed into the dark cloud of failure. For my daily workout routine in those days, I just beat myself up. I'd failed. Failed to finish college. Failed at my music career. Everything in my life was wrong. When I was around my friends who had their degrees, I felt inferior. In my mind, I told myself I'd never amount to anything. I had fallen into a small-minded mentality. I was embracing the "poor me, I didn't graduate from college so I guess this is the miserable life I'm destined for" mentality. Not exactly a Pat Williams's daughter theme song, but it's a fact that we all listen to voices we shouldn't from time to time. Instead of hearing my dad's encouraging messages, I believed the voice that told me I was a nobody. I was buying into the lie that I could never make it. Never do that! It's *not* true.

Then one day I came across a quote in an article that hit me right between the eyes. It read, "No one can go back and make a brand-new start; anyone can start from now and make a brand-new ending." It was almost as if my dad were right there in the room. I don't know if he ever said those words exactly, but it was the heart of his message: "You can do it. It's never too late to start." After all, my dad didn't start running marathons until he was in his fifties!

I chewed on that thought until it literally changed my life. I realized I had been beating myself up over something I had complete control to fix. How silly I'd been! That quote made me realize I could start from "now" and rewrite my script, complete with a brand-new ending. Another way Dad puts it is, "Start where you are, use what you have, and do what you can." No one else was going to do it for me, but I saw in that moment that I could do it for myself. It's not as if a person can't go back to school, after all. So I re-enrolled at the University of Florida and gladly made the two-hour commute from Orlando to Gainesville for a year, while also working full-time in the real estate business. The following spring, I graduated with a degree in broadcast journalism. Boy, was I proud! And so was Dad.

Start where you are, use what you have, do what you can.

My dad has always had a way of encouraging us to think big—really big. Maybe you've heard that every success story begins with a "BHAG," or a "Big, Hairy, Audacious Goal," an acronym coined by Jim Collins and Jerry Porras in their book *Built to Last: Successful Habits of Visionary Companies* (HarperCollins, 1997). I'm pretty sure if you could look up that phrase in the dictionary, you'd see my dad's picture next to it.

He has never allowed us to limit our thinking to the "so high and no more" mentality.

When we were growing up, Dad had a fun game he'd play with us. No matter what our interest du jour was, he would immediately go to the top of that particular field and begin pumping us up about becoming "the next" whoever. Take my childhood interest in gymnastics, for example. Because I would have been the right age to compete in the 1996 Olympics, Dad talked nonstop about me going to the Olympics in Atlanta and becoming "the next" Mary Lou Retton or Shannon Miller. It didn't happen, but it sure wasn't Dad's fault.

In college, when I showed an interest in the news industry and decided to major in broadcast journalism, he was sure I was going to be "the next" Katie Couric. When I won the Miss University of Florida pageant, he was already talking about me being "the next" Miss America. And with singing, of course I would be "the next" Shania Twain or Faith Hill.

Obviously, I didn't become the next Mary Lou Retton, or the next Katie Couric, or the next Miss America. It's not so much about *achieving* every goal you set your mind on, but about *having* a goal to begin with. It's about having someone to look up to, a bar that's been raised above your head that you must reach for. There's another old saying—that if you never try, you'll certainly never know what you could have done.

There was something magical about the way Dad ended those childhood conversations, and it's the point of this little vignette. He'd say, "Karyn, you could be the next Mary Lou Retton—*if* you want to!"

There's no reason any of us can't make it to the top of our chosen fields—*if* we want to. Yes, it requires hard work—some blood, sweat, and tears. But the victory begins in our minds. Simply *believing we can* is half the battle!

Parents, there's another valuable lesson here. You see, my dad never made us feel like we *had* to be the best for him to love us. But he encouraged us to think big, take life by the throat, and view ourselves as the best. Most little girls will not compete in the Olympics, even if they begin gymnastics lessons at five years old. But how many youngsters have quit before they could ever find out because they didn't have the right encouragement at home?

Think big!

Because of the "think big" mentality Dad instilled in me, I went into every gymnastics practice with a winning attitude. Every time I ran down the runway toward the vault, I could hear crowds cheering and see the perfect "10" score revealed as I accepted my gold medal. In college, I approached every news story I wrote as if I were delivering it on the *Today Show* sitting next to Matt Lauer. And now, every time I pick up a microphone to sing, I see myself as Celine Dion singing to an arena of thousands. It might sound Pollyannaish to you, but I refuse to limit my thinking into "so high and no more."

I admit I've been a victim of the "what if I can't do it?"

mentality a time or two. We all do it. We fear failure, so we stay inside, never venturing out of the "safe zone." "What if I sit down at the piano after all these years and it doesn't come back to me?" "What if I open my mouth to sing and the wrong note comes out and I'm embarrassed?" *So what?* Nobody's perfect. The only way you'll figure out what you love is by daring to put yourself out there and mess up a time or two. God can't steer a parked car! Life is short. Swing for the fences. Dare to screw up. Hey—dare to screw up *big-time*. Just dare to live!

Pat's Lesson

I was never more proud of Karyn than the day I watched her walk across the stage at the 2004 University of Florida graduation ceremony. For three years, I had witnessed my daughter's growing frustration over the fact that she hadn't completed her college degree. Every once in a while, I'd gently nudge. "When are you planning on returning?" I'd ask. And when she was ready, she did. Of course, it was more difficult returning to college as a twenty-four-year-old, but she completed twenty-one credit hours her last semester and continued to work full-time in real estate while she did it. As her dad, I was pleased to see her decide not to let past decisions stand in the way of future glory.

What's your dream? We all have one, but most of us end up giving up on them somewhere along the way. Life happens, obstacles seem too hard to overcome, and we end up choosing to live a life of quiet frustration, never living to our full potential, never accomplishing what we could have, always limited by a mind-set that says "so high and no more."

My kids always loved hearing about how fleas are trained. At the fair there's a flea exhibit that has trained fleas jumping up and down in a glass canister, and there's no lid. So the obvious question is "why don't they fly away?"

The flea trainer explains that he puts them in a glass with a lid on it and they keep jumping up and down hitting their little flea brains on the top. After enough Excedrin experiences, they stop jumping so high. At that point the trainer can remove the lid, and forevermore those fleas will stay contained, no longer by a plastic lid on top, but by a mind-set that says "so high and no more."

Unfortunately, like those fleas, there are a lot of people running around inside plastic containers with no lid. We buy into the lie that we can't do something, and live a life—like the fleas—of quiet frustration, never living to our full potential, never accomplishing what we could have, and always limited by a mind-set that says "so high and no more."

I spoke in Mexico City in October 2008, and had a wonderful guide name José. José was just twenty-one years old, and his English was broken. But his meaning came through loud and clear when he said, remarking on the contrast between wealth and poverty, "When you are at the bottom it's important to learn from it, so that when you are back on top, you'll be a whole lot smarter." I thought to myself—José could shout this one.

We only get this one chance. How tragic it is—and unnecessary—if we miss what we've been put here to do. I was torn when Karyn told my wife, Ruth, and me she believed her time had come to go to Nashville and pursue her goals. I didn't want to hear it at first. I didn't want my baby girl flying so far from our nest. But I've seen how determined she is, and I knew she just had to do it. We must all dare to live large! Our hope is that Karyn's story will inspire other young readers to grab the golden ring and make their own dreams come true.

Living big requires taking some risks. And that leads to another key quality: you've got to fight through your fears. People who dare to live big get knots in their stomach, their hearts are pounding, their palms get sweaty—believe me. They've got doubts. These people are not superhuman, but in every case they fight through the fear. They battle that negativity in their mind. They plow through the barriers, because there's an inner quality that simply will not yield. They *will* not be denied.

I don't want to get to the end of life saying, "There were so many things I wanted to do, but I never could pull the trigger. I was just too scared. I just could not get over the hurdle."

Henry David Thoreau once wrote, "Most men lead lives of quiet desperation and go to the grave with the song still in them." I want to sing every note of my song while I'm here. Don't you?

THE TAKEAWAY

God did not make us for the ordinary; he made us for the extraordinary.

But most of us live so far below that. Just "okay" is never what he had in mind for us.

Don't rob yourself of an amazing life—go for it. You're not too old; it's not too hard.

Start taking baby steps toward what it is you want most out of life. No one is going to do it for you. It's entirely up to you!

Dare to live big.

CHAPTER 8

Life Is About "Collecting People"

W hile I was still in high school, Dad gave me a copy of Harvey Mackay's book, *Dig Your Well Before You're Thirsty* (Doubleday, 1997). I have to be honest and say I didn't read it all the way through at the time, but the title of that book has always stayed with me. Dig your well *before* you're thirsty. In other words, take the time to prepare yourself for what is to come. I've heard nutritionists say over and over, "If you wait until you're dying of thirst to drink water, more than likely you're already dehydrated. Begin drinking water before you feel thirsty." The same concept applies to building and maintaining relationships.

As I became an adult and entered the business world, Dad began saying, "Everyone is in the people business, Karyn. You've got to be 'collecting people.'" And I knew what he meant, because I'd watched him do it all my life. That's not something you need a butterfly net or an eBay account for; rather, it's something that naturally occurs when you treat others with kindness and respect, as my dad has always done, and as we discussed in Chapter 3. When you do that, it comes back to you in the form of doors that open. Some people call it networking. I call it relationship building. Either way, it's what happens when other people you've "collected" push the doors open for you.

It has amazed me to hear Dad call a friend or business acquaintance from five, ten, or even fifteen years ago and strike up a conversation as if no time has gone by. He's the master of maintaining relationships, and I've been blessed to be his student. Because of his example, I've grown to understand the importance of relationships and collecting people. Yes, it's true that every now and then we hear those rare stories of an artist being "discovered" by some fluke, but nine times out of ten, it was a facilitated introduction that got them through the door. "Discoveries" like that only come from establishing the right relationships. When it was time to flex my own wings, I knew if I wanted to have any chance at a career in music, I needed to begin introducing myself immediately to people in Nashville. So that's just what I did.

I threw myself completely into the music community and went to work building relationships. I went to every event I could. I put myself in positions to meet other musicians and began singing with them. I asked for introductions. I learned to recognize when I was getting a "polite" blow-off, and I "politely" refused to accept it. When someone said, "I'll have 'my guy' call you," I'd immediately respond with, "That's wonderful, thank you so much. Would you mind giving me his number so I can follow up with him as well?" I boldly walked through every single door that opened before me.

Dad had said over and over, "Go meet everyone you can, Karyn! Go knock on Alan Jackson's door and introduce yourself to Denise!" "Oh right, Dad," I'd say, "security would be hauling me off before I could finish knocking!" We'd laugh about it on the phone, but I understood his point. *Don't be afraid.* And you know what? His "no fear" approach to relationships has inspired me. Although I haven't gone so far as to knock on the Jacksons' door yet, I have thrown myself with reckless abandon outside my comfort zone, and it has paid off—big-time. Follow me on my journey through my first six months in Nashville, and I'll show you what I mean.

Be a people collector!

I'd lived in Nashville about four months before going home to Orlando to spend Thanksgiving with my family. While out with some friends one night, I ran into an old friend and he began asking how things were going. At the end of that conversation, he said, "You know, I ought to introduce you to my friend Pat Armstrong. He has some ties to the music industry and I think it would be helpful for you to talk to him."

"Sounds great!" I replied, and a door opened.

As it turns out, I had met Pat a few years before, so I took my dad's "live bold" advice and called him up to reintroduce myself.

After we'd chatted for a while, Pat said, "You know, you ought to meet my friend Charlie Allen. He's a heck of a songwriter and a wonderful singer."

"Sounds great!" I replied, and another door opened.

Pat connected me to Charlie, who said at the end of our first conversation, "You know, you ought to meet my friend Brian White." I immediately thought he was referring to Bryan White, the country artist. But he explained, "No, my friend Brian is a songwriter and producer."

"Sounds great!" I replied. I had no idea in that moment that the drawbridge to my personal castle was about to come down.

It turned out Brian is not just a songwriter—he is a number one *smash hit* songwriter. To date, he has eleven number one hits to his credit and has had songs recorded by Avalon, Point of Grace, Jody McBrayer, Michael English, the Martins, Neil McCoy, Trace Adkins, and Rodney Atkins's 2008 chart-topper (five weeks at number one) "Watching You."

Charlie set up a lunch date for the three of us for the following Friday—a meeting that would dramatically change the course of my life in Nashville. Brian and I immediately struck up a friendship and began writing together. In no time at all, he began introducing me to other writers, producers, music industry executives, and friends. He even put me in a room to write with other hit songwriters. Because of that relationship, I've had the opportunity to share a stage with writers like Arlos Smith (who wrote "Mayberry" for Rascal Flatts), Bill Shore

and David Wills (who wrote "Wild Horses" for Garth Brooks),
Barry Dean (who wrote "God's Will" for Martina McBride),
Steve Dean (who has written for everyone
from Reba to George Strait), and most
recently, I had the privilege of sharing an   *Doors open*
evening with Hall of Fame country   *when other people*
music legend Tom T. Hall.   *you've "collected"*

Thanks to that series of connections,   *push them open*
I've experienced the Dove Awards, the   *for you.*
American Country Music (ACM) Awards
in Las Vegas, and I've been introduced to the
heads of publishing companies who have the ability to offer a
publishing deal that would allow me to write music full-time—
and I hadn't even *known* I wanted to be a songwriter! It's amazing what a few good "people connections" can show you about
yourself. Within five months of meeting Brian, I found myself
with a cut on a major record project and songs "on hold" for
the likes of Martina McBride, Kellie Pickler, and Sara Evans.

God's not surprised by any of this, but to me it's a dream—
and it all happened in less than a year. If I ever start feeling
frustrated, I remind myself to look back at how far I've come.
The Bible says that if we delight ourselves in the Lord, he will
give us the desires of our hearts (Psalm 37:4). I believe that is
a twofold promise: first, he plants the desires in us, and second,
he leads us to the place where we can take hold of them to
achieve our life purpose and glorify him in the process. God

used my dad to teach me to be a people collector, and as a result of my willingness to say, "Sounds great!" he has truly given me the desires of my heart. And it all goes back to my friend in Orlando who knew a guy, who knew a guy, who knew a guy. . . .

Please don't misunderstand: this message isn't about "using people." It's about recognizing that the Lord places people in your path to help you further your dreams and carry out his plan for your life. God really does have a purpose for your life, and it's one only you can fulfill. But first, you've got to give God your dreams. He'll help you make them come true—usually in ways you would never expect—and he'll let the people you've collected along the way be the ones to open the doors.

Pat's Lesson

Ever since Karyn moved to Nashville, I've been amazed to discover that almost everyone I meet knows somebody who lives in Nashville. "Oh, I've got a son in Nashville!" or "My cousin Sue lives there." The entire world seems to be descending on Nashville. So I answer, "My daughter Karyn lives there. Maybe the two of them can get together. I'm sure they would get on famously!" And I'll ask for their information or tell them how to reach her. As a result, I have a little ritual that Karyn has come to expect. At least twice a month, I'll send her a package with business cards or notes from people I've met who live in or around Nashville. It's my part in helping her "collect" people. I smile every time she calls and tells me she just had coffee with someone I've introduced her to.

Have you ever thought of yourself as a people collector? If you haven't, perhaps you should. I once heard Matthias Schmelz, entrepreneur and author of *The Millionaire Maker* (Fenix Lusitana, Ltd., 2007), tell a radio interviewer about the daily habits of wealthy people, using Donald Trump as an example.

Schmelz said that Trump gets to the office at about 9:00 AM every day and picks up the phone, first thing. He doesn't stop to check his e-mail or surf the Internet—he just starts calling people. Before noon he has talked to about fifty people. And then after lunch, he starts all over again with the calls. Trump and thousands of Trump wannabes believe in the power of networking. Collecting people—business contacts to them—matters in the world of the power-lunch eaters. The truth is, people matter in every single profession and walk of life.

Whether you are an architect, an athlete, a writer, or a dog trainer—people are what life is ultimately all about. There's a lot of jabber today about people being the cause of Earth's problems. And yes, we all need to live responsibly. But we've got to understand that people are pretty much what makes the world go 'round.

Truly wealthy people have more contacts in their phone book than cash in their wallet. The wise person knows this and invests time every day into building relationships—with family members, friends, colleagues, and neighbors.

In sales, trainers teach you to picture your ultimate goal and then work backward, setting short-term goals to reach your personal finish line. What is your ultimate goal in life?

I've often thought about my funeral. Now I'm not trying to be morbid here—I have a point. When I picture my funeral, I always see a church filled with lots and lots of people, rejoicing over a life well lived. That is my ultimate goal. Now if I work backward from that point, it means I need to be developing relationships and "collecting people" every day. If I don't, that church will be pretty empty. Author Harvey Mackay calls it "digging your well before you're thirsty."

Think about the millions upon millions of dollars spent on advertising every year—commercials, billboards, magazine ads, the list goes on and on. But sit with business leaders and ask them one simple question: "What's the most effective way of developing new business?" Here is what they will say: "Relationships, referrals, and word of mouth."

Think about the last time you got a huge opportunity to do something. It doesn't matter what it was—a new job, a chance to work in a great ministry at your church, or an invitation to speak somewhere. How did that opportunity come your way? More than likely that opportunity knocked when someone else opened the door for you.

I once read that one of President George H. W. Bush's friends described him as a man who "collects people." I like that statement. I like it when people say that about me.

The greatest joys in my life are the relationships I've built during a career of almost fifty years in sports. I've always told my children to seek people out. Go introduce yourself. Tell them hello. Ask them a question—particularly if you run into somebody of note. You may have nothing more than a thirty-second encounter with them, but that experience will brush up against your life forever. My children respond, "I didn't want to bother them" or "Oh, I was too nervous." But those are opportunities that may never come again. Above all, when you have one of those encounters with a notable person, make sure you're ready with a question.

As an author, I spend a lot of time interviewing people for books I am working on. Several years ago, while working on the book *How to Be Like Walt Disney* (HCI, 2004), I was stunned time and again by the "coincidental" meetings I had with people who'd known Walt. There was definitely Disney magic in the air. Just as the book was about to go to press, I was attending a book show in Chicago and sitting in the "green room" before speaking when who should breeze through but Mary Poppins herself! Julie Andrews stood before me in all her glory, giving me a moment to ask, "What do you most remember about Walt Disney?" Her face lit up as she replied, "Oh, Pat, his sparkling eyes!" And she was whisked away to another engagement.

Once I was invited to attend the twenty-fifth anniversary of the Washington Speakers Bureau, an organization I work for. So I went to the event and was able to meet and talk to everyone from Lou Holtz to Madeleine Albright to television personalities—they were all there. At the dessert reception, I looked across the chocolate éclairs, and who was reaching down for one but General Colin Powell. My son Bobby, twenty-seven at the time, had just started a managing career in the Washington Nationals farm system. Knowing General Powell is a baseball fan, I went over and introduced myself. I told him about Bobby and asked, "General Powell, what advice would you give him?" Over the dessert table, Powell replied, "Tell your son to take care of the troops." Then he paused and said, "Tell him to keep his mouth shut and do his job." He started to walk away, then leaned back and said, "And don't worry about your next job." And he was gone. I raced over to get a cocktail napkin to write down what Powell had said. I titled it, "General Colin Powell on leadership, in twenty seconds." You just never know when those moments will occur. Be ready and don't let them slip away. I promise you'll regret it if you do.

Woody Hayes, the great Ohio State football coach, said, "You win with people." I would say that in the game of life, that's even more true. It's all about the people in your life. How many have you collected, my friend? It's a lifelong pursuit, and well worth it.

THE TAKEAWAY

Make it a point to be a people collector every day of your life. That way, you'll be digging your well before you're thirsty, and you'll never run dry.

**Life is about
"collecting people"!**

CHAPTER 9

There Are No Giants
Out There

My heart raced as the music began playing at the MGM Grand in Las Vegas, introducing the Forty-third Academy of Country Music Awards, held on May 20, 2008. While it would be broadcast and watched by millions of people across the country, I was actually *there!* And completely starstruck. Just before the show went live to television, in they all walked to take their seats—George Strait, Carrie Underwood, Brad Paisley, Kenny Chesney, Taylor Swift, Rodney Atkins. *Wow!* I thought. *These are all my heroes—* next to my dad, of course.

But I reminded myself of an experience I'd had just a few short months before. When I first moved to Nashville, I immediately got in touch with Tim Akers, an old friend who is an incredibly talented piano player. He told me that he had landed a gig playing on the road for LeAnn Rimes. How cool, I thought. Not long after that, Tim called and said LeAnn was playing at the symphony hall in downtown Nashville, and would I like to come? "Would I like to come? Of course!" What

I didn't realize then was that Tim was planning on bringing me backstage. As he walked me into the "green room," I couldn't believe my eyes. There sat LeAnn Rimes, her feet propped up on a piano bench, wearing sweatpants, with her hair tied up in a ponytail! I got to hang out with LeAnn for a few minutes before her show. I walked away realizing what a normal person she is. Then I asked myself, *what else would she be?*

It's so easy to feel intimidated, isn't it? As young people, we tend to look at people in high positions as if they are larger than life. A couple of years ago, I took a job that challenged me to reach for a whole new level. It required me to call on large Fortune 500 companies, traveling all over the East Coast to run business meetings with their leadership teams. Wow—did I feel inadequate! The night before I started the job, I sat on the couch with my best friend, tears pouring down my face. I felt completely overwhelmed just thinking about what was ahead of me. What if I didn't know what to say? What if I opened my mouth and nothing came out? What if I got nervous and lost my train of thought during a meeting? What if they weren't nice to me? Have you ever been chased by the "what if" monsters? They are merciless.

It was during that season of my life that Dad began saying to me, "Karyn, there are no giants out there." I'm so glad he used that word "giants." We've all been told at least once not to feel intimidated by others, but for some reason "giants" put it into perspective for me.

I thought of the story in the Bible where the Israelites sent in spies to scout out the Promised Land before they went in. The reports they brought back were interpreted by some as saying it was "mission impossible" to even try to go in there. "There are giants in the land!" they cried out in alarm. There weren't, of course. But even if there had been, they'd already forgotten the power of God, who had parted the Red Sea and drowned the Pharaoh's soldiers. Did they think they were alone?

And then there was the story of David, the little shepherd boy who fearlessly went up against the giant Goliath in an effort to free his Israelite companions from Philistine intimidation. How Goliath laughed at this child. Who was he kidding? But when David let fly the well-aimed pebble from his trusty slingshot, the laughter stopped. Goliath came crashing down and the victory was won. That little shepherd boy went on to become king of Israel. David knew the secret: there are no giants, save God alone.

No one is larger than life!

People haven't changed much in the last few thousand years. Today, we tend to look at those in high positions as if they're larger than life—as if they are truly giants. We feel small in their presence, overwhelmed, and inadequate. But guess what? That "giant" sitting across the desk from you was once a college student. And he was probably a "lowly" intern not that many years ago, too. Think about it this way—everybody was a "nobody" before they got to be a "somebody." These so-called "giants" are actually everyday people just like you. They put on their pajamas and climb into bed just like everybody else. Their hair is a mess when they wake up in the morning, and they even have dragon breath before they brush their teeth, just like the rest of us. After work, they're as exhausted as you are and can hardly wait to go home and crash on the couch with the remote in their hands.

These word pictures might sound laughable, but when I'm in the presence of someone who might intimidate me, it helps a lot to think about all the mundane things they do every day. Like running into your favorite professor, the one you absolutely idolize, at the grocery store. You mean *she* needs to eat and buy toilet paper, too? Or running into your boss at the movies with his wife and kids. You mean *he* doesn't live at the office? It helps me to create a mental picture of them as "everyday" people and not giants at all.

While in Orlando for a visit one November, I sat down with one of my favorite people in the whole world, David Uth, the pastor of my church, First Baptist Orlando. He asked how things were going and I excitedly began to ramble off stories about my progress in building relationships with people in Nashville and about meetings I had coming up with some music executives. He prayed with me and then said something that painted a wonderful picture in my mind. Pastor David said, "Karyn, I want you to remember that the Scripture says the 'king's heart is a stream of water in the hand of the Lord;

he turns it wherever he will'" (Proverbs 21:1 English Standard Version).

I've tucked his piece of advice in my "back pocket"—the one I keep in the back of my mind—and pull it out every time I am walking into a meeting with one of those not-so-big "giants." To calm my nerves, I've developed a little mental game, based on what Pastor David said, that's really a great strategy. I picture that "giant's" heart cupped in Jesus's hands. It helps me keep perspective on who is *really* in control.

No matter how powerful they seem, don't let yourself be demoralized by people who look like giants to you. They're just normal people who have worked hard to get where they are. In truth, they're really only a few steps ahead of you. Instead of being intimidated by them, study them. Learn what has made them successful. Study the things you like—or don't like—about them. Maybe even invite them to lunch or ask them to mentor you. It will help you develop into the leader *you* want to become one day.

> *The king's heart is a stream of water in the hand of the Lord; he turns it wherever he will.*
> —Proverbs 21:1 (English Standard Version)

Pat's Lesson

I completely understand how Karyn felt at that country music show—surrounded by all the people whose lives had lit up her own for so many years. I've been in professional sports for more that forty years and have written more than fifty books, and I still find myself reeling at the star power of some of the people with whom I have the privilege of associating.

In one of our family's favorite Mickey Mouse features, Mickey plays the part of a medieval tailor who one day manages to get the upper hand on seven annoying giant flies—only to have the king mistakenly think he is able to slay real giants. At first, Mickey is terrified when the king appoints him to rid the town of a genuinely menacing giant. But once he's offered the hand of the fair Princess Minnie as a reward, our intrepid hero becomes a mouse on a mission. Largely because of his determination—certainly not his strength or skill—Mickey eventually brings the town giant to his knees and discovers that the big galoot wasn't so tough after all.

Are there days when it looks like you can never get over that mountain or that you'll never defeat the giants in your land? We all have seasons like that. Sometimes life just seems too much to handle. How will we ever get through this trial?

But what happens to a mountain when you're looking

down on it from an airplane? And what happens to that giant after he has fallen? It's all a matter of perspective. Once you know there are no giants—only people who think more of themselves than they ought—then you know you have ultimately nothing to fear.

Determination is a key quality for taking down giants. Decide in your mind you will never quit, never—not for anything.

We've focused a lot in this chapter on the giants who might be out to squash us or trip us up in some way, but there are also the giants we idolize and admire—the people who intimidate us. They look the same from that airplane window—not like giants at all. And I've come to know firsthand that many of them can be pretty regular people if you give them half a chance.

Our writing partner in this book told us about the time she, too, met Carol Lawrence. As a Disney performer many years ago, she had a unique opportunity to entertain Carol's children and afterward spent some time chatting with Carol and her then-husband, actor/singer Robert Goulet. "I was a starstruck college kid," Peggy said, "but I'll never forget how comfortable Ms. Lawrence made me feel. She didn't focus on herself but on me! Where was I going to school? What did I hope to become one day? Even Robert Goulet made me feel I was among friends."

I mentioned my son Bobby in the last chapter. Bobby is now the farm director for the Washington Nationals. He's been in professional baseball since he was twenty-two years old. I can remember in my early days being dazzled when I was suddenly surrounded by my heroes, just as Bobby is today. You're in the business you've admired all your life and now working with and against people whose autographs you were seeking not many years earlier. Suddenly you're in the same field with them. So I counsel my son, "Bobby, they're famous people, but they're not superhuman. Believe it or not," I tell him, "in many ways you're sharper and more capable than they are." "No!" he whispers in disbelief, but I assure him, "Yes, you are! You may not have had their playing career, but you've got skills they'll never have. Don't sell yourself short. That doesn't mean you have to be cocky or arrogant, but just know that deep down within, you are just as capable as they are."

I got my first NBA general manager job in Chicago at the age of twenty-nine. Suddenly I was doing business and matching wits with people like the great Red Auerbach of the Celtics and other legendary names—people I'd admired for years! I was so starstruck, I had to pinch myself. I kept saying to myself, *Act like you know what you're doing. Pretend you've been doing this your whole life. Don't let 'em see your knees shaking.*

So many people in our lives, both the good and the bad, will seem like intimidating giants, but the fact is they are just people like you and like me. We all pull our basketball shorts up the same way. For Karyn, it's learning that even country stars need to buy toilet paper now and then. Whoever it is that makes your knees knock, remember that they are mere mortals who once had knocking knees, too, just like you.

THE TAKEAWAY

Remember: There are no giants—only a few people who think that's what they are. No matter what valley you walk through or how big the opposing army might seem, hold your head high with confidence . . . you are never, never alone.

There are no giants out there!

CHAPTER 10

The World Will
Take Care of the Jerks

That new job I mentioned—the one I cried over the night before I started it—required me to administer franchise operations in several markets along the East Coast. It was a big challenge for me at twenty-seven to "oversee" franchises owned by men who were twice my age and much more experienced in business than I. The job also required me to run business meetings with CEO-level executives and presidents of companies. There was definitely major-league pressure in my life.

At the end of one particularly tough day, I found myself feeling especially discouraged. Not sure what to do, I called the man I knew would have an answer and a word of encouragement—my dad. I'm sure I said something like, "Why do they think they can treat me like that?" And Dad calmly replied, "Honey, just do your job and go about your business. The world will take care of the jerks."

By the summer of 2007, I was especially glad I had that advice from Dad tucked away in my heart. Still living near my family in Orlando, I'd been dreaming about a possible move to Nashville, but that dream was still in its misty stages, very loose. After all, I had a good job, I was making good money—I didn't *need* to go anywhere.

So one day in June, I got up, packed my usual lunch, climbed into my car and switched on the radio to my favorite country station like always, and took the same route I always drove to work. It was an ordinary day, at least for the first few hours. Midmorning, my boss called a company-wide meeting—something he rarely did in this small organization. What was up? When he came into the room, his face visibly sagged. We could see that his heart was heavy.

"Guys," he began, "I can't believe what I'm about to say. . . ." We scooted up in our chairs and listened in stunned silence as he explained that the company was closing down. The investor money had dried up. And then the worst—there was no money to pay the bills, including our salaries. Since the next day would have been payday, he was telling us we had basically donated the last two weeks of our lives.

Naturally, we were all blown away. He assured us, of course, that he would do everything he could to get our salaries paid within a reasonable amount of time. Thousands upon thousands of dollars in unpaid commissions were owed to the sales staff in particular—including me. We were assured it would all get worked out. And we believed him.

I packed up my office and wondered, *what's next?* After putting my boxes into the car, I called Dad to tell him what had happened. Since the owner of the company was a personal friend of Dad's, it was a double whammy for him to learn his friend was going through this tough situation.

The next few months were difficult financially, to say the least. I took the company's closing as my signal that it was time to pack up and head to Nashville. If you've ever moved before, you know that moving is expensive. If it weren't enough to have to pay first and last month's rent and deposit plus hiring a moving van, add in all the unexpected expenses and you can drain a bank account real quick. Because I had already been thinking about this move, I'd been careful with my money. But I had also been planning on having all the money owed to me—money I had earned.

Everyone is dealing with something!

I should have been okay, but I wasn't. Instead, I heard myself crying on the phone one night to Dad about having only sixteen dollars left in my bank account. "Sixty dollars?" he said. "No, Dad. S-i-x-t-e-e-n!" I wailed. I hated admitting that to him because I firmly believed in being responsible for myself. It felt as if, in spite of all that I had done right, the rug had been pulled out from under me.

Now, I don't have a hot temper. Not even close. Nor do I instinctively want to "get back" at people. It's just not the way I'm made. But the owner of the particular market I worked in is a well-known celebrity. I confess having one or two thoughts about exposing the situation and embarrassing him. And who would have blamed me? They'd made money from my sales but were using every excuse they could think of not to pay me for my hard work. But my dad's words kept ringing in my ears: "Keep your mouth shut and go about your business, Karyn. The world will take care of the jerks."

Several months later, I learned that my former boss had been forced to declare both personal and professional bankruptcy. At this printing, it's been more than two years since the company closed down. I have not seen one penny of the money that was owed to me, in spite of having gone directly to the franchise owner who benefited from my sales. But by God's grace and my dad's advice, I've let it all go. When I think of all he lost, I honestly have compassion for my former boss. So when I see a situation I know is not fair—and they happen often in this world—I hear that deep male voice I love so much saying, "Karyn, just keep your mouth shut and let things play out."

Ever had someone say something about you that wasn't true? We've all had incidents like that. It seems to be part of life. Jealousy gets the best of a girl who sees her "best friend" getting close with someone else. Or your boyfriend's ex approaches you with "dirt" from his past in an effort to stir up trouble in your relationship. Our first instincts are to scream, "That's not true! Why are you lying?"

One such unfortunate incident happened to me not long ago while on a weekend visit in Orlando. Thankfully, I was with my family and they helped me walk through all of the emotions, and allowed me to talk it out. I dealt with it and eventually let it go, but it was hard. Words can paint powerful pictures that are hard to erase from your mind. It only takes a *few* sentences from a miserable, jealous person to do a lot of damage. As Dad would say, "Your tongue is the most powerful muscle you have."

Keep your mouth shut and let things play out.

That Sunday morning, I headed back to Nashville, still raw and hurt by the situation. I flipped through radio stations as I drove, and naturally I caught a few sermons. As I'd lose a station's signal, I'd tune in to another one, and at one spot on the dial I heard the strains of a familiar, beloved hymn. I smiled while listening to "Turn Your Eyes upon Jesus," a song that I'd both heard and sung so many times. Then came the line, "and the things of earth will grow strangely dim in the light of his glory and grace." The meaning of that line came in crystal clear in that moment, as I held it up against the painful experience I'd just been through. It was as if the Lord was sending *that* message directly to *me* through that crackly radio station in my car, just when I needed it most. How it comforted me to see the hugeness of my situation shrink in the light of "his glory and grace." I reflected on the fact that one day, when I meet him face-to-face, these things of earth that seem like such a big deal right now *really will* grow dim.

We all face situations where we would love to see someone who's done us wrong "get theirs." But vengeance, the Scriptures say, belongs to the Lord. I'm sure there is a lifetime of lessons ahead of me, but I've learned God is far better able to handle both the anger and the results. So whatever you may have experienced in life, and no matter how unfair it might seem, know that someday it will all be made even. You may not live to see it—that's entirely possible—but if you take my dad's advice, to keep your mouth shut and let things play out, you'll have peace in your heart and a perspective far bigger than the momentary problems you may face.

I've mentioned elsewhere in this book our counselor friend in Orlando, Dwight Bain. "Uncle Dwight," as I call him, taught a Sunday school class at First Baptist Orlando for many years before opening his own private counseling practice. He was a wonderful teacher, and his Sunday school class became so popular that on any given week he'd have from 200 to 300 people attending. One day, he made everyone turn and say to the person on their right, *"You've got issues!"* It was hysterical.

Even though it was a humorous moment, Uncle Dwight is right. Life is hard, and every one of us has "issues." I learned a long time ago never to judge another person too quickly, because you never know what they're going through. The lady in the grocery line who seems a little impatient could be rushing to get to her son's birthday party at school. Or the man on the highway driving like a maniac may have just learned his wife was admitted to the hospital. You just *never know* what people are going through. Have you ever had an acquaintance or coworker who didn't seem like "themselves" for a while, only to find out months later they were going through a bitter divorce? That has happened to me more times than I'd like to admit. Way too often, people *clam up* when they should be *opening up*, so we can't always know what they're going through.

One day when we were on vacation at the beach a few years ago, one of my sisters met a guy. They chatted a little bit, exchanged phone numbers and e-mails, and then we went home to Orlando. When she didn't hear from him, she got a little upset. Why didn't he call or write? The following year, we were back at the same beach—and there he was. It turned out that right after that meeting the summer before, his little five-year-old daughter was diagnosed with non-Hodgkin's lymphoma. No wonder he hadn't called!

My point is that we tend to immediately take things personally and lash out, thinking, *I can't believe that person would do that to me!* In reality, we're not victims at all. People are going through things every day that we don't know about.

I visited a church called "The Anchor" in Nashville not long ago with some friends. It was a small church consisting of a predominantly younger demographic. They had just returned from a weeklong retreat, and before the pastor got up to preach, he asked for a few people who had been at this retreat to get up and share their experience.

What hit me was that every single person who stood up to share that night said a different version of the same thing. The basic message was that they had been hurting inside—big-time. One woman had experienced two miscarriages in the last nine months. Another guy shared about his experience with some abuse and how he has been trying to break free from the pain. There was nothing on their faces that said, "I'm hurting." They looked like anyone we'd meet in the mall, or the grocery story, or even sitting in traffic. I'm telling this story simply to prove the point that you *never* know what someone's going through.

We've used the word "jerks" in this chapter with our tongues planted slightly in our cheeks to prove a point. I don't think anyone wakes up and says, "I think I'll be a complete jerk to everyone I come in contact with today!" I think most people wake up with good intentions, but sometimes out-of-control situations in our lives get the best of us and we react in ways that aren't exactly flattering. That's something to think about the next time you're tempted to jump to conclusions. Step back and cut people a little slack.

One last note: just as we were finishing the writing of this book, I found myself laid off, once again, from my most recent job. After all was said and done, I told Dad I had e-mailed my boss, my boss's boss, and his boss's boss to thank them for the opportunity to work with them and learn from them. Dad said,

"Good job, Karyn. I'm glad you did that. Class always separates itself in times like these." When it's your turn—and it will be at some time—I hope you keep that in mind, because it's true. In a world all too often full of jerks, class always separates itself. Like cream, it rises to the top.

Pat's Lesson

Years ago the fishermen working in the cod business had a problem. They would capture the fish and ship them off to market, but en route the fish would die, which ruined the quality of the fish. Then somebody had the bright idea to put a certain type of catfish—the catfish that happened to be the cod's chief enemy, the number one jerk in the cod's life—into the water with the cod. Having the catfish in the tank kept the cod moving, racing around for their lives. As a result, they made it to their destinations still hanging on.

So perhaps there is a certain kind of catfish in your tank—let's call him a jerk—stirring up your life and causing you all sorts of problems. I've had them in my life—some owners, some teams I've been involved with, some employees, managers, or coaches that have been part of my teams. Oh, they were difficult. Oh, how I wanted them not to be there. But in retrospect, I learned a great deal from working with difficult people. I'm stronger and more capable as a result of having had those catfish in my tank.

One of the things I've learned is to always try to set a good example for those around you. Parents, your children are going to be dealing with jerks their whole lives. Some of the stories Karyn has told here reminded me of incidents I'd long since forgotten, but her testimony is powerful. Our kids are watching how we treat people in tough situations.

There was one particularly difficult period in my life when I had to make a conscious effort to set a good example for my children in how I treated their mother after she filed for divorce. It was a very tough time in all our lives, but I was determined that my children see that you *can* act respectfully and in a dignified manner through complicated, unpleasant, and even intensely painful times.

Karyn has had setbacks in her life. She's had adversities, disappointments, and failures, as we all have. I've always told her to turn them into positives, to realize that everybody on planet Earth has just come out of a storm, or you're in the middle of a storm, or you're headed into a storm. The most important thing during the storm is to keep thinking, *What can I learn from this? What can I take from it on the other side of the storm? How can I be more effective, more capable, better able to help other people?* In the middle of a personal storm years ago while living in Chicago, my pastor, Warren Wiersbe, at Chicago's Moody Church, said to me, "Don't waste your sufferings." That's what he said, right in the middle of all the stuff I was in—and I still think it's the most important piece of advice I've ever received.

There's a human tendency to think that when we're dealing with a jerk or when we fall into some trouble, a superhero or fairy godmother will come along soon and just whisk it all away. But even the king of contemporary fairy tales, Walt Disney himself, believed adversity could be a good thing. Walt suffered a lot of setbacks on his way to success, and looking back on it all, this is what he said: "All the adversity I've had in my life, all my troubles and obstacles, have strengthened me. You may not realize it when it happens, but a kick in the teeth may be the best thing in the world for you."

Not long ago, I heard Pastor David Uth at First Baptist Orlando preach a sermon about the time when Peter was "defending" Jesus. Peter took a sword and went after one of the Lord's accusers, intending to cut his head off. The man turned as Peter approached him and lost only an ear. Pastor David asked, "What did that accomplish for Peter? What's it doing for you? Put your sword away, folks. It's never going to work for you. You may feel it does, but at the end of the day you're better off putting your sword away." Like Peter, we're better off to lay down our swords and let God deal with those we feel have done us wrong. Maybe you needed that kick in the teeth, just like Walt.

There's no doubt about it—this world has no shortage of jerks and tough situations, but it is simply not our job to get revenge. I've learned it's important to treat people as you want to be treated yourself—including those people who are doing their level best to ruin your day, or even your life. There's a Scripture I turn to time and time again for instruction, and it says this: "If your enemies are hungry, feed them. If they are thirsty, give them something to drink. In doing this, you will heap burning coals of shame on their heads" (Romans 12:20 [New Living Testament]). I know it sounds completely contradictory—why would we want to be nice to people who are out to hurt us? But the Scripture is clear, and the clue to its meaning is in that last of Paul's lines—when we repay evil with kindness, the "jerks" are often made to feel ashamed of their bad behavior, or at the very least they are exposed for what they are. However it happens, the world *will* take care of the jerks.

THE TAKEAWAY

Next time you want to point a finger, step back and realize that you may not know the whole story.

Cut the "jerks" in your life a little slack.

You never know what's really going on in someone's life.

**The world will take care
of the jerks!**

Make Good Decisions

When Dad was just a little guy, artist Norman Rockwell was painting covers for the old *Saturday Evening Post* magazine. One particular cover must have caught his three-year-old eye and inspired the household he would one day lead, because Rockwell's now-famous "Freedom from Want" definitely portrays the Williams family at Christmastime.

On Christmas Eve 2004, we were all home for the holidays. As we caught up on one another's lives, our mouths were watering over the yummy smells of roast turkey, mashed potatoes, and pumpkin pie wafting from the kitchen. So when the dinner bell finally rang, it was more like a referee's whistle. Not surprisingly, we found a book at each place setting—Andy Stanley's newest release, *The Best Question Ever* (Multnomah Books, 2004). Immediately there was a "buzz" in our dining room. "What's the answer?" one of us said. "Wait, what's the question?" piped another.

Then Dad stood up and presented the challenge (can you tell by now he likes to challenge us kids?). "The first person to read this book and figure out what the 'question' is gets a fifty-dollar gift certificate to Fleming's restaurant."

I immediately went to work. I read late into the night. I got up and began reading first thing the next morning. I was *determined* to win that gift certificate. Finally around lunchtime, I called Dad. "I've got it," I shouted. "I know what it is!"

According to Andy Stanley, "the best question ever" is simply this: "What is the *wise* thing for *me* to do?" Stanley says we should ask this question in light of our past experiences and where we want to go in the future. The answer we come up with may not always be the "fun" or "popular" thing to do, and it's not based on what's best for someone else. But when faced with any situation—large or small—it's a question we should ask ourselves individually.

I have always appreciated Dad's ability to drive home a point using humor or real-life examples like that book. Like this statement he was always making when we would ask to stay up for just one more hour, "Nothing good happens after ten o'clock!" I hate to say it, but I've learned he's right—again! So when Dad presented us with Andy Stanley's golden question, I knew it was something to treasure. From the moment I first read the book, I have loved it. Without a doubt, it's since been applied to every area of my life. It's that important. When I'm at the mall considering a purchase, I ask myself, *What's the wise thing for me to do right now?* When I want to go hang out with friends but I feel a cold coming on and know I should go home, I ask myself, *What's the wise thing for me to do right now?* When I've seen something that doesn't seem fair and I want to open my big mouth (and probably stick my foot in it), I ask myself, *What's the wise thing for me to do right now?* I'm telling you—asking this simple question in every circumstance will change your life.

Nothing is more critical for young people like you and me than making wise choices about our actions. Have you seen the news lately? I don't know about you, but I sure don't want my life or that of any one of my little nieces and nephews to turn out like some of the teen queens we see gracing the covers of magazines these days. I've heard the term "train wreck" used, but in my opinion, the train wrecks look good in comparison to some of these young women. At least the train wrecks happen by accident! Decide what kind of reputation you want to have, and then ask yourself, "Are my words and actions portraying that person?"

Use your head!

I've adopted a little ritual when making decisions in my life. I've decided that if I have to stop and ask myself if what I'm considering is a good decision or not, then it's probably not. In other words, if I'm writing an e-mail and I think "Hmm, I wonder if I should say that?" chances are, I probably shouldn't. In those moments, I can hear my dad's voice saying, "*Use your head*, Karyn. Make good decisions!"

The other thing I hear my dad saying is, "Relax, give it time."
Many bad decisions are made out of haste. I've heard more than
a few of my friends admit, "If I had dated him longer, I never
would have married him." Time isn't *always* a luxury when
making decisions, but whenever it's available to you—take it,
use it, embrace it. Time really is your best friend when it comes
to making good decisions. Most of the time if you'll walk away
for a while and then come back to the question, the right decision for your life is staring you right in the face.

One of Dad's heroes is Abraham Lincoln, who had a favorite
method for venting his personal frustrations and heartaches (of
which there were many). He would sit down and write a letter
to the person who'd tweaked him. When he was done, he would
tear it up and throw it away. The letters never
got mailed! Clearly, Abraham Lincoln
knew how to make the best decision ever.
What's the wise thing for me to do right now?
—Andy Stanley
I've followed this advice with every
decision I've made since reading that
Andy Stanley book, and I can tell you
without a doubt, this is probably the simplest but most powerful piece of advice I
can offer you. *Every* decision, large or small, will
come back to "haunt" you in some way. The only way to be sure
you won't mind that "ghost's" company is to make decisions you
can be proud of later in life. Many times, a good decision will
seem ordinary. No fireworks go off, no booming voice comes

down from heaven saying, "Good job, little one—you've made the right call." No, it's usually a quiet choice that *you* know is best for your life.

One night, at dinner with friends, I heard about an accident that had taken place with a young woman they knew. Intoxicated well beyond the legal limit, she made the foolish decision to get behind the wheel of her car. The police said she was driving between eighty and one hundred miles per hour when she slammed into a guardrail, ejecting herself across the road where she landed in a tree. She was not wearing her seat belt. For the next few days, her life hung in the balance at a hospital near Nashville. She was in a coma for five of these days. Eventually, she opened her eyes. At this writing the extent of the damage done to this young girl's body is still not certain, but one thing is sure—she will never be the same. These same friends then told me about a twenty-five-year-old young man whose pancreas was about to be removed because of damage done during his teens—by drinking alcohol. Both of these regrettable outcomes started with one decision—to take one sip from an alcoholic drink. Was it worth it?

One of the biggest failings we have is that so many of us get caught up in the now and don't stop to consider "down the road." But think back on some of the things to which you couldn't say "no." Is there a choice you now regret making? Maybe even that extra fudge on the sundae last weekend that's got your favorite MEKs a little too tight? You get the point.

This chapter wouldn't be complete without discussing a touchy subject—private decisions made regarding your personal life. Now hear me—those are *your* decisions, yes. But, please, please take a minute to read and process this statement: *EVERY decision you make behind closed doors will affect you down the road.* How will you feel when you've just walked down the aisle in a beautiful white dress, only to head off to your honeymoon suite knowing that you've already given away your most precious jewel—behind the bleachers of your high school football stadium? Worth it?

Think about how your decisions will affect *other* people. In other words, *you've* saved yourself for marriage. You finally meet the woman of your dreams and decide to get married, only to find out she had a reputation for "sleeping around" in her younger days. Or you develop a relationship with a woman who has already been affected by the pain of adultery, only to have to divulge to her that you made some poor decisions in a previous marriage yourself. Worth it?

We have become a society of "I want what I want, and I want it now!" I say—*come on!* Cool your jets a little and realize that if it's worth having, it will wait for you to be ready. We need to start using our brains and acting with more respect— toward others and ourselves.

Make a decision that you will rise above temptation and conduct yourself with dignity. Decide how you will handle situations *before* the heat of passion takes over. It's a heck of a lot easier to get off a train before it gets going than it is to jump out and try to stop it once it's speeding down the track. You usually end up with a train wreck and a whole lot of hurt people. Please be careful. Make wise decisions now and you'll have less to regret later on. I hope you'll make every choice from now on by asking yourself the best question ever.

Note to parents whose kids are still at home: I've heard it said that a young person's frontal lobe doesn't fully develop until early adulthood. I'm not going to get scientific on you here, but after some research, I've found this to be true. The frontal lobe of our brains controls judgment, impulse control, problem solving, and social behavior. So what does this mean? Well, some would say not to allow young people to make any key decisions for themselves until the age of thirty! Of course, that's more than a little extreme, but the point is that as kids, we act like we've got it all together, when in reality, we need our parents' help—all the way to age thirty and beyond.

As kids, we need you to set healthy boundaries for us that will teach us good decision making! In E. D. Hill's new book, *I'm Not Your Friend, I'm Your Parent* (Thomas Nelson, 2008), she says, "We have a responsibility to our children not to give rights and control to them before we equip them to handle it." We need you to guide us and help us, not allow us to run free and screw up our lives. Sometimes, we honestly don't know better (even though we think we do). You've lived more years than us. The phrase "older and wiser" wasn't just pulled out of thin air; there's truth behind it! We're going to buck against you. We're maybe even going to claim that you're wrong and you don't know what you're talking about. But one day, down the road a way, we will realize that you did know all along, just as I am now understanding about my one-and-only dad.

Pat's Lesson

As Karyn shares with me her stories about life in Nashville, I remind her over and over, "Keep your nose clean. Live your life as if you're Reba McEntire, and everything you're doing could be exposed." We see it every day—news about someone prominent who made a bad decision at some time in their past. A tabloid picks it up, and before you know it, at least a dozen lives are ruined.

On a recent trip to California, Ruth and I visited the Reagan Library in Simi Valley. As we wandered the rows of displays that vividly told this U.S. president's life story, we were struck by one realization. It was as if Reagan knew he was destined for greatness because he groomed himself for it every step of the way. Was his life perfect? Of course not. But he kept himself above ground level and lived like a future president. Who do you want to become? Why not start living as if you already have that role? You can do it by always asking yourself "the best question ever."

Here's something you young readers have got to realize: your teen years are *not* disconnected from the rest of your life. Some of my kids thought they were on a teenage island, just floating out there, and that this time had no relationship to the rest of their life. But the truth is everything you do through your high school years is going to totally affect what kind of life you have. The better your decisions as a young person, the better chance you have for success in life. You make bad decisions as a young person, and you'll be battling upstream forever.

A couple of my kids decided to drop out of high school, but now they realize it was a horrible mistake. They're finally going to college, deep into their twenties, and they've got to work at the same time—and it's a lot more complicated. No matter what your friends think, you've got to play your own game, not theirs. I urge you to realize that what you do today does matter tomorrow.

What if you are one day a candidate for office? Are you living a life you'd want exposed? If the media is able to dig up everything now, by the time you're tossing your hat in the ring, their techniques and tactics will only be better. Please, please, please—think about the choices you're making every day.

One year when sixteen of my children were all teenagers at the same time, I was often asked, "Are there some common traits you see with these children? They come from nations all over the world and have different backgrounds, but is there anything they all share in common?" I replied that I'd observed two common attitudes:

1. Everything in their life was related to how *cool* it was. That was the plumb line. And the most *uncool* thing I noticed with my teenagers was to be too passionate, too excited, too enthusiastic about *anything*, because that would not appear to be cool to their friends. But I have learned that the world belongs to passionate people, people who wake up every day excited about what they're doing, people who are totally enthused and engaged.

2. The second thing I found with my teenagers was that their definition of work and my definition were not even close. I heard them talking often about how *hard* they were working in school, and how *hard* they were working to keep their rooms clean, and how *hard* they were working in sports. And I chuckled to myself, thinking, *we're not on the same page here*. We have totally opposite views of what hard work is.

One choice in particular that I've always stressed to the children is that of always being honest. I tell them, "More than anything, always tell the truth. When you get out in the real world, if people doubt your word one time, you're in *deep* trouble. If they doubt it twice—you've had it. You're going to have to pack up all your possessions, move across the country, start all over again, and hope that nobody finds out. That's how important it is that people know you as an honest person, and that what you say is always the truth, every time, without exception." I can't think of anything more important. It's not always easy, but truly wise people have learned that the truth will find you—*every time.*

"Integrity" is another key value I impressed upon Karyn and the other children. It comes from the root word *integer,* which, of course, leads to our word integrated. An integrated society is "one" society. A person of integrity has a consistency to their life. I used to say to Karyn, "Be the same at the football game as you are at church on Sunday; be the same at school on Monday as you would be at home on Sunday night; be the same with your friends as you would be with your family. In other words, don't be a chameleon. We don't need five versions of yourself depending on who you're with. One consistent version— that's the earmark of people of integrity. There's a completeness, a wholeness to their lives. I like how former U.S. Senator Alan Simpson put it, "If you have integrity, nothing else matters. If you don't have integrity, nothing else matters."

Not long ago, I was visiting with Ken Whitten, who is Coach Tony Dungy's pastor in Tampa, Florida. Ken told me, "The tongue in Tony Dungy's mouth always points in the same direction as the tongue in his shoes." In other words, Tony's talk and walk are lined up with each other.

When I think of the word "integrity," I immediately see one man's face in my mind's eye: that of former Philadelphia 76ers star Bobby Jones. I never met a man who was more humble or trustworthy, or whose life was more consistently good. I've often said that if I were to pick one man for young people to model their lives after, it would be Bobby Jones.

One night when we were playing the San Antonio Spurs, Jones was involved in a play that left the ball heading out of bounds. Because Bobby's body position cut off the referee's view, when the ref picked up the ball, he whispered, "Bobby, did you touch it?" Surprised by the question, Bobby answered, "No, I didn't touch it." "All right," the ref replied and called out, "red ball!" That meant the '76ers' retained possession of the ball.

Two weeks later, we happened to be playing a game in Philadelphia, and there was that same referee. This time, a similar play occurred, only it *did* go out of bounds off Jones's hands. Again, the ref asked him, "Bobby, did you touch it?" And Bobby answered, "Yes, I did." Coach Billy Cunningham heard every word and was decidedly not happy. "Bobby!" he shouted, stamping his feet. "Let the ref make the call. That's his job!" Later on, Bobby told me why he'd been so honest, even though it resulted in a call that cost our team. "My integrity," he said, "is not worth sacrificing for a possession."

We all need to be more like Bobby Jones—conscious of making good decisions every day of our lives—choosing to tell the truth and to be men and women of integrity. Those are the only decisions we won't waste time regretting. As humorist Will Rogers once said, "Live so that you wouldn't be ashamed to sell the family parrot to the town gossip."

It is so rewarding to realize your kids are getting those lessons. When my son Michael was nineeen, we were having lunch one day when he surprised me by using the word "integrity." So I asked him, "Michael, what does integrity mean to you?" He replied, "Honesty, with a little oomph."

The most critical time to make those good decisions is when we are young. It's those key choices that form the foundation—the launching pad as it were—for the rocket ride of our lives.

THE TAKEAWAY

Get into the habit of asking yourself, "What is the wise thing for me to do?"

It is the simplest but single most important piece of advice I've ever received, and I guarantee it will change the way you approach decisions in your life.

You'll never regret them—

Make good decisions!

READER/CUSTOMER CARE SURVEY

HEFG

We care about your opinions! Please take a moment to fill out our online Reader Survey at **http://survey.hcibooks.com**.
As a **"THANK YOU"** you will receive a **VALUABLE INSTANT COUPON** towards future book purchases
as well as a **SPECIAL GIFT** available only online! Or, you may mail this card back to us.

(PLEASE PRINT IN ALL CAPS)

First Name		MI.	Last Name

Address			City

State	Zip	Email

1. Gender
☐ Female ☐ Male

2. Age
☐ 8 or younger
☐ 9-12 ☐ 13-16
☐ 17-20 ☐ 21-30
☐ 31+

3. Did you receive this book as a gift?
☐ Yes ☐ No

4. Annual Household Income
☐ under $25,000
☐ $25,000 - $34,999
☐ $35,000 - $49,999
☐ $50,000 - $74,999
☐ over $75,000

5. What are the ages of the children living in your house?
☐ 0 - 14 ☐ 15+

6. Marital Status
☐ Single
☐ Married
☐ Divorced
☐ Widowed

7. How did you find out about the book?
(please choose one)
☐ Recommendation
☐ Store Display
☐ Online
☐ Catalog/Mailing
☐ Interview/Review

8. Where do you usually buy books?
(please choose one)
☐ Bookstore
☐ Online
☐ Book Club/Mail Order
☐ Price Club (Sam's Club, Costco's, etc.)
☐ Retail Store (Target, Wal-Mart, etc.)

9. What subject do you enjoy reading about the most?
(please choose one)
☐ Parenting/Family
☐ Relationships
☐ Recovery/Addictions
☐ Health/Nutrition
☐ Christianity
☐ Spirituality/Inspiration
☐ Business Self-help
☐ Women's Issues
☐ Sports

10. What attracts you most to a book?
(please choose one)
☐ Title
☐ Cover Design
☐ Author
☐ Content

TAPE IN MIDDLE; DO NOT STAPLE

FOLD HERE

Comments

CHAPTER 12

Are You a Leader
or a Follower?

When I was born, I had two older brothers, Jimmy and Bobby, already waiting for me. I loved my big brothers, but boy, did I want some sisters. When I was four, my wish came true—and the Williams family adoption story began. Two little Korean girls joined our family in September 1983. I was beyond thrilled!

Sarah, Andrea, and I immediately bonded, like sisters do, and created wonderful memories growing up. One of my favorites is the time I decided to play "hairdresser" to Sarah, butchering her long, beautiful black hair. I'll never forget hearing her cry, "I look like a boy!" I'll also never forget the look on my parents' faces. Oh my—thank goodness it grew back, and quickly. I have watched these two beautiful little girls grow into strong, confident women who I am proud to call my sisters.

In 2004, Sarah found out she was pregnant. My first niece was on her way! Laila Michelle Kindy was born the day after Hurricane Charley ripped through central Florida. Because no one had power after that hot, muggy, and devastating storm, we were thrilled to head to the hospital that afternoon—both to welcome Laila and to enjoy the hospital's air conditioning.

When I was home visiting my family not long ago, I noticed a little game Sarah had begun playing with her now four-year-old Laila. Oddly enough, it's a game that reminds me of something my dad would have done with us (I guess Sarah has had a few "takeaways" of her own, huh?). Sarah gets Laila's attention and asks her daughter, "Laila, are you a leader or a follower?" To which Laila proudly responds, "I'm a l-e-a-d-e-r, Mommy!" The first time I heard this, I nearly fell out of my chair. All of our lives we've been hearing Dad talk about leadership. And here was the evidence, being faithfully passed on to yet another generation.

The truth is that right from the beginning (and with no prejudice whatsoever on my part), Laila has shown leadership qualities. She is incredibly smart, knows exactly what she wants, and is bold about making it happen—much to the frustration of her parents at times. At two-and-a-half years old, Laila began referring to her younger cousins as "the children." And whenever she is playing with one of the younger kids, at some point we know we will hear Laila's voice, loud and proud, "Here—let me *show* you!" I am so proud of my sister for encouraging her daughter to think like a leader right from the start.

I am a firm believer that leadership can be a learned skill. Birth order may play a part, or you may naturally have a more outgoing personality than others, but true leadership skills can be acquired and polished.

Dad has a funny illustration to prove this point (you guessed it, my firm belief came from him). He says, "I don't think that doctors hold up newborn babies and say, 'Yep, looks like we've got a leader here!'" I agree with him. Leadership skills are learned over time, and improved with experience. Leaders bring vision, ideas, and energy to every environment they're in. They're not afraid to voice their ideas and opinions. They're also open-minded enough to listen to others' ideas and opinions. Leaders understand the importance of making good decisions and are constantly steering themselves toward wise decisions for their own lives. Once we're aware of these skills, we can develop them.

No one is a born leader.

As "big sis" to fourteen younger brothers and sisters, I was entrusted with leadership roles from a young age. Then as I got into high school, I adopted the famous "Pat Williams mentality" of taking on everything in sight. I took honors classes, was the captain of my cheerleading squad, president of our Fellowship of Christian Athletes (FCA) chapter, carried the lead role in our high school musical, and was vice president of my senior class. Just before graduation, I found myself at my doctor's office thinking I had mononucleosis. He jokingly said to me, "Slow down, Karyn, you don't have to save the world on your own. That's a concept your dad still hasn't learned!"

During the Miss Florida competition, a curveball was thrown my way that offered me a rare opportunity to stand up for what I believed in on a large scale, and in front of a large audience. It was a true test of my sister Sarah's game—are you a leader or a follower?

I have never been more prepared for anything in my entire life than I was in the summer of 2000 for the Miss Florida pageant. I threw myself into voice lessons, interview coaching, and twice-a-day workouts. If someone was going to beat me, it was going to be because they truly deserved it, not because I wasn't prepared.

The week of preliminary competition couldn't have gone any better. I felt wonderful about my one-on-one interview with the judges. They had asked great questions that allowed me to talk about my platform—international adoption. With fourteen brothers and sisters added to our family from around the world, it was a subject I could talk about for hours. Earlier in the week, I had nailed my song during the preliminary competition, taking home the talent award that night, which I knew would help my overall scores. My spirits were soaring going into the final night of competition. We did the opening number and then it was time to announce the top ten contestants who would continue on. They began calling names. Number six, number seven, number eight. I was starting to sweat, when I finally heard, "Karyn Williams!" at number nine out of ten names. Whew! I got ready for a whirlwind night as we flew through each phase of the competition one last time for the judges before they made their final decision.

As you can imagine, my large family was in the audience on the edge of their seats the entire time. Each time I came out onto the stage, they went bonkers, screaming and hollering. It was such a thrill! Then came time for the announcement of the top five.

I held my breath.

This time, out of the five names my name was called fifth. What were these judges trying to do, give me a heart attack? There was one last hurdle we had to jump through before the big announcement was made and the crown would be given to the new Miss Florida—the brief interview on the couch.

I changed into my interview suit once again and joined the other four contestants on the sofa. Keep in mind that *this* was the portion of the competition I was ready for. I had gone through numerous mock interviews that my coach had set up, where the "judges" had grilled me to pieces. I had met with my pastor at the time, Jim Henry, to discuss how to answer controversial questions from a Christian perspective without alienating everyone else. We'd discussed everything from the death penalty, to abortion, to gays in the military. My dad's famous "article cutting" to stay up on current events never came in more handy than it did during the weeks leading up to the competition. Yes—I was ready for whatever question they were going to throw out at me. Or so I thought.

Since I was fifth out of the five, I had time to gauge how tough these questions would be. So I sat back and listened to the questions being fired at the first four contestants.

"Should there be a minimum age requirement on obtaining a marriage license?" *Hmm*, I thought, *that was kind of a softball compared to what I've prepared for.*

Next question, "How do you feel about school uniforms?" *Wow*, I said to myself, *this is going to be easier than I thought.*

The questions continued in the same fashion.

"How do you feel about hazing on college campuses?"

"What can we do to instill more confidence in our young people?"

I was next. I took a deep breath and got ready.

They handed me the microphone and I turned to our host, Wayne Brady, for my question.

"Karyn, recently the Southern Baptist Convention decided to ban women as pastors. Do you feel this is direct prejudice against women?"

I was stunned. I couldn't move, couldn't speak, and certainly didn't know what to say. I heard a collective gasp go out over the audience, followed by whispered murmurs. I wished with all my might that I was one of those contestants on the game shows that got to call a friend. I'd have given anything in that moment to be able to turn to my dad in the front row and ask for his advice—I desperately needed a lifeline!

This decision by the Southern Baptist Convention had just

taken place on the previous Monday, and this was Saturday night—just five nights later. Because of the schedule during the week of competition, it was impossible to have any time to watch the news, read the paper, or stay on top of the news. So I had no idea that this had even happened, let alone anticipate that I would be required to answer a question theologians have debated for years.

And then I realized God was giving me an opportunity. I could stand up as a leader for what I believed, or I could slink back and do the "easy" thing as a follower and answer the question in a way I thought they might want. The stakes were pretty high. If I answered the question "their way," I'd probably win the pageant, be crowned Miss Florida, and be on my way to Atlantic City to compete for the coveted title of Miss America.

Leadership skills can be learned!

What should I do?

I slowly began my answer, "I agree with the decision. . . ."

A second round of gasps went through the Hard Rock Live in Orlando.

I continued by explaining why I agreed with the decision; that the Bible clearly states the man is to lead the church and I wasn't going to argue with that.

I handed the microphone back feeling completely deflated. I wanted to cut a hole in the stage, climb down inside, and never come out. How could they bring religion into this? *My* religion! What made me feel worse was the knowledge that each question had been chosen specifically for each girl. This wasn't a random question chosen out of a hat. They had intentionally put me on the spot, and it wasn't fair.

But I knew I had done *everything* in my power to win the competition that night. If God wanted me to win and be given a larger platform from which to speak, then I knew he would work it out regardless of the controversial question I'd been asked. It was out of my hands now, and the decision was up to the judges.

Fourth runner-up was announced, then third.

I was still standing.

They announced the second runner-up, and I became one of two girls still in the running for the title of Miss Florida.

I grabbed my competitor's hand and wished her luck as we awaited the final announcement.

Wayne Brady began, "The first runner-up is . . . Miss University of Florida, Karyn Williams!"

I saw my sister Caroline, who was sitting in the front row, jump up when they called out my name. It took everyone a split second to realize that it meant that I was in *second* place. I didn't win.

As soon as the pageant was over, I was overrun by reporters from newspapers and radio stations across Orlando. They all wanted an interview, and they all had one question: "Do you think that question cost you the crown?"

I truly didn't know what to say, but I didn't have long to think about it because one of the competition officials wisely led me away before I could answer. I was approached by hundreds of people that night who said, "We are so proud of what you did!"

As I stood there—still in my gown and holding that big bouquet of flowers, I have to be honest and tell you that my first thought was, *What did I do? What is everyone so proud of me for?* I was just answering the question from an honest place in my heart. I wasn't trying to create controversy or be some kind of hero.

The next morning the *Orlando Sentinel* ran a front-page picture of me with an article about the controversial question and a summary of how the pageant had turned out. The headline read, "MISS UF AGREES—NO WOMEN PASTORS."

"Oh boy," I thought. "Let the firestorm begin. . . ." And it did.

Friends and family of the girl who won wrote to the "Ticked Off" section of the newspaper and complained about why the article wasn't about her—the winner.

I heard the controversy discussed on the afternoon talk shows. I was interviewed the next morning on XL 106.7, one of the largest radio stations in central Florida. They were very gracious and conducted a wonderful interview.

That week I received a handwritten note from my pastor, Brother Jim, that read, "Karyn, I heard how tall you stood at the

Miss Florida pageant and I am so proud of you!" The following Sunday, he brought me onstage at church and explained the story to the congregation.

I was overwhelmed by the whole situation. I just kept thinking, *What in the world did I do that was so great that everyone's making such a big deal out of it?*

Looking back now, I realize that everything I've ever known about being a leader came out in that moment. At a women's pageant, I'm sure the answer I gave was not the one they wanted to hear. I had a choice. I could have chosen the politically correct answer they probably wanted. But I instinctively chose to answer in a way that was not popular, not easy, and created quite a local controversy.

Here's the bottom line—we are all faced with a choice every time we enter into a situation. The choice is am I going to be a leader or a follower? I'm sorry if my next statement bursts your bubble, but let me go ahead and tell you that it *ain't always easy* taking the "leader" route. In fact, sometimes it's downright hard. It's hard to walk away from your friends when they're all doing something you know is wrong. It's hard—at *any* age—to stand up for what's right around your peers.

But I encourage you to begin developing leadership skills now. You never know when you will be faced with your "what's it gonna be" moment. When it does, there's no time to deliberate and decide how you're going to react.

When you find yourself in a situation like the one I was in

that night—in the spotlight and on the spot for an answer—I encourage you to take the high road. Stand tall. Listen to your gut. Hold firm to your beliefs and do what you know is right. Let's all follow young Laila's lead and practice being leaders instead of followers.

Pat's Lesson

I was devastated when Karyn didn't win Miss Florida. I mean, *devastated!* Before the competition was over, in my mind she was heading to Atlantic City, and I could see her being crowned Miss America. I know, I know—I'm a little biased. But the truth is, she should have won. She owned the stage, and the crowd loved her. She had the highest scores in all of the preliminary competitions, and she won the interview portion, which counts for almost half of the total score. It was obvious the title was hers. My heart sank as I heard Wayne Brady read that question to her. *Oh no,* I thought. *Either way she goes with this—she's dead!*

For weeks afterward, I would corner Karyn in the house and *beg* her to compete again the following year. But she graciously accepted her defeat—much more graciously than I—and moved on. She took what happened better than any of us and finally made me realize that she saw it not as a failure, but as a rare chance to show the world who she really was. In truth, I was proud, for it was everything I've taught her about standing up and being a leader.

I'm always talking to my children about leadership. I'm fascinated with the topic, because everything rises and falls on leadership. It always has, and it always will.

When our youngest son, Alan, was in high school, I had an interesting experience with him. Alan is a good kid—a goof-off, but a good kid. He loves sports and was playing on the basketball team at his school. I kept stressing to Alan that he needed to be a leader and set a good example for the other kids at his school. Alan wanted no part of that. It's tough to be a leader when you also want to be a goof-off. You can't do both. One day an excited Alan climbed into the car with me. "Dad!" he said, "Guess what?" I said, "Alan, fill me in." "The coach named me captain of the basketball team today." "Wow!" I said, "Alan, that's awesome." After a pause, I said, "You know what that makes you, Alan?" Silence. Finally, he squeaked, "A leader?"

I've learned with young people that they need to view leadership as a three-legged stool. The first leg is seeing yourself as a leader; the second is preparing yourself to lead; and the third, is stepping up and actually leading when the opportunity presents itself.

For forty-seven years I've been in leadership positions in professional athletics. I'm also a collector of leadership books. I have more than five hundred of them in my leadership library at home and I've read them all. Both my experience and my research have convinced me it takes seven key ingredients to achieve outstanding leadership:

1. **Vision:** Leadership is always about the future. Visionary leaders see farther than others, they see more than others, and they see before others.

2. **Communication:** You've got to be able to communicate your vision. You do this by communicating optimism, hope, inspiration, and motivation, and you must be able to communicate verbally. To a large degree, leaders lead by their voice.

3. **People skills:** Outstanding leaders have a heart for people. They care about others; they have empathy and love for people.

4. **Character:** You can only go as high on the leadership ladder as your character will permit. I'm talking about old-fashioned values here like honesty, integrity, respect, and humility.

5. **Competence:** Leaders are good at what they do. They take their God-given leadership skills and are always working to improve them.

6. **Boldness:** At the end of the day leaders have to make decisions. They gather information and they ponder carefully, but they must decide the best course of action. More harm is done by making no decision than by making the wrong decision.

7. **A Serving Heart:** I love the first sentence of Rick Warren's bestselling book, *The Purpose Driven Life*

(Zondrvan, 2002). It says, "It's not about you." Serving-hearted leaders have always known that.

You may not have the natural gift of leadership, but I've heard it said—and I believe it—that we are all leaders in some way. Someone somewhere is watching us, looking up to us, and expecting us to model correct behavior for them. Now that you've got those seven keys, you are responsible for them. Please take them, apply them to your life, and use them well.

THE TAKEAWAY

*Don't be afraid to stand up for what you know is right—even if it means losing a longed-for job or title. Don't be a follower—**be a leader**. Show others the right way to live.*

Challenge yourself every day:

Are you a leader or a follower?

CHAPTER 13

You're Always Building
Your Résumé

During my first year selling residential real estate, I caught a big break. I developed a relationship with a family who ended up purchasing two homes from me that together totaled almost three million dollars in sales. It resulted in a *very* large payday for me, and boy was I excited! *This real estate thing is a piece of cake,* I thought.

Not long after that, I was having lunch with my family when Dad struck up a conversation about my schedule following the close of those two sales. I talked myself up, telling Dad I was staying busy, hungry for more sales. I almost believed it myself. But truthfully, I was feeling a little too proud of myself for having so much success with such a short track record.

> *Don't rest on your laurels!*

"It seems to me you're resting on your laurels a bit," Dad said to me that day. I did my best to talk my way out of it, but inside I knew Dad was right. You know that feeling—just about the time you've got your balloon blown up all the way, someone comes along with the straight pin of truth and pops it. I'd been thinking I was hot stuff, when really I was just getting started.

I have since adopted the mentality of my former business associate, longtime NFL great, quarterback Ron Jaworski, who said, "I will not allow anyone to outwork me." I can't stop and rest for one second if I want to stay on top. Now that I am pursuing in earnest my true passion for singing and songwriting, I have to remind myself every day that the competition is fierce. There is always going to be someone nipping at my heels ready to take my spot if I'm not at the top of my game. I remember Dad saying once about his job, "All that matters at the end of the day is what's in the 'W' column. It's wins versus losses, and my industry will surely replace me if I don't have enough 'Ws.'"

Dad recently interviewed author David Buckley regarding his biography of singer Elton John (*Elton: The Biography* [Chicago Review Press, 2007]). Dad asked Buckley what keeps Elton John striving so hard, even at age sixty. Buckley replied, "He's still trying to get another hit, and he's competing against entertainers who are a third his age." Like John, we've all got to be continually pressing toward the goal.

My friend Brian White, who wrote the number one smash country song "Watching You" for Rodney Atkins, says, "I don't want to be the person that people talk about, saying, 'Isn't he that *one* guy who had that *one* hit a few years ago?' I want to follow it up with hit after hit after hit!" True to his word, he hits the ground running every morning, continually asking, "Who can I write with today who will challenge me to be a better songwriter?" Even after writing plenty of hit songs, I have never once heard him say, "I've made it, and I'm a big deal!"

I've mentioned elsewhere that Dad is a marathon runner—and he's got me doing it, too. To date, I have completed nine marathons, and while finishing them is exhilarating, believe me, they are *not* fun. There are two reasons I run marathons—to practice my "not quitting" skills (you'll read about those in Chapter 16), and to build my résumé. I'm going after the "wow" factor in my life, and the only way to do that is to keep building my experiences, education, and skills. You'd be surprised how many people say "wow" when they hear that I run marathons. Is there anything you're doing that adds a "wow" factor to your life? If not, I'm not saying it has to be marathon running, but find something you love doing that makes other people sit up and take notice. It can only make your life richer. Not only will that "wow" enhance your life, but it will likely attract a few interesting and wonderful people into your inner circle.

If you've already got your college degree, think about going for the next one. Or look for ways to become certified or accredited, or whatever the next level is in your field of work. Whether or not you build your résumé through jobs and career moves, you can strengthen it by taking classes, attending seminars, joining professional organizations, getting published, public speaking, and many other ways.

Recently, Dad and I were having a conversation about my singing career, and I said, "When I make it. . . ." Dad stopped me immediately and said, "Karyn, don't ever fall into the mind-set of having 'made it.' That's when it becomes too easy to get lazy."

Dad's right again (isn't he always?). We should always be playing offense and strategizing ways to improve, to challenge ourselves, and to figure out ways to get better at whatever it is we're doing.

> *Don't ever fall into the mind-set of having "made it."*

I've met a lot of successful people in my life, and there's one thing I've observed about them: I call it an either/or mentality. They *either* have a humble, never-quit attitude that says, "Yes, I've done well, but I'm not letting it go to my head," *or* they have a spirit of "entitlement" that shouts, "I've made it. I don't need to work quite so hard anymore. I'm a big deal!" Ever noticed what a big turnoff it is to be around people like that?

These kinds of people are everywhere. It doesn't matter what industry, whether it's sports, music, real estate, publishing, or any other. The truth is, you will never fully "arrive" in this life. We are meant to be works in progress, and as such we will always be paying our dues. The best way to do that is to never stop learning, never stop reaching higher. I can hear my dad's voice now: "You've got to keep gaining experience, Karyn! You'll never be finished paying your dues!"

One day Dad said to me, "I'm a better speaker today than I was a month ago. And I'll be a better speaker next month than I am today." I was really affected by that statement. My dad views every speech he does as practice—an opportunity to build his résumé and hone his craft. Part of it goes back to that "enjoy your life" thing we talked about earlier. But the truth is, my dad is of the mentality that he will never fully "arrive" in this life, and he does everything he can to steadily improve his skills.

Determine to be proactive. You know how to build your iTunes library, don't you? It works the same way! What can you add to your résumé today? And what can you add that makes people say "wow" about you?

Pat's Lesson

Businessman Clarence B. Jones, a former speechwriter for and longtime associate of Dr. Martin Luther King Jr., observed, "An employer is essentially renting your knowledge in the hopes of making himself or his company more successful. There are no freebies here in the real world; jobs are strictly a business proposition." What an interesting perspective—that an employer is renting your knowledge. Working with that analogy, you could offer "affordable housing" or you can keep building your résumé and become a high-rent penthouse! I know which neighborhood I want to live in.

Every time Karyn says she wants to run another marathon with me, I am one proud dad. I know full well that what she's volunteering for is not fun. A marathon is not what most kids would choose for an outing with Dad. Plain and simple, these contests are about as grueling on the body as anything I can possibly think of or have ever done. But with each marathon we knock down, we've both built a little more into our résumés.

Some years ago, I was sitting in a San Diego Padres game with my friend, pastor and author David Jeremiah. David authors books, has a national radio and a national television show—he's all over the place. I said, "David, when are you going to give up your pastorate and go into retirement?" He said, "You never want to be a former anything." He went on, "People forget you real quick. Everything I do out of the pulpit triggers my writing, and it's the basis of my radio and television ministries. Besides," he said, "I'm still working to learn this craft."

I'm a great admirer of Coach John Wooden, the UCLA coaching legend who's now ninety-eight years old. Coach has done his best writing since his ninetieth birthday—six books that are absolutely terrific. So at ninety-eight, he's still learning, still looking to improve, still building his résumé. You never are there—you never have arrived.

If you want something badly enough, you've got to persevere to reach it—and that means hard work, nonstop. Walt Disney called it "stick-to-it-ivity." I call it "never giving up," and it's a major reason why I advocate continuing your education. Keep pumping for that promotion, carving away at your craft—whatever that is in your own life. Don't fall into the "I've made it" mentality. My kids hear that from me quite a bit, and by now they understand that, for Dad, life is all about going after the "wow" factor. The only way I can do that is to continually challenge myself. At age sixty-nine my speaking career continues to grow, but the competition is more intense than ever. I've got to keep building my résumé if I am to stay ahead of the game.

What is it for you? How will you continue to light up the room every time you walk into it? I believe it's what we all long to do, and the only way to keep the wattage from burning out is to never stop building that résumé. This life, after all, is only a rehearsal for eternity. My goal is to get it right before the executive director ultimately calls out, "Cut and print!"

THE TAKEAWAY

Go for the "wow" factor with your résumé. Imagine you're being introduced to a group of people you'd like to impress. What do you want to be said about you? Keep building on that message.

**You're always building
your résumé!**

CHAPTER 14

Don't Spend Any Money
Until You're Thirty

Y ou know those commercials that talk about all the things you can buy with a dollar? I found myself trying to remember what those things were during a particularly rough financial period in my life. Dad had always taught us to be responsible for ourselves and to manage our money wisely, but due to circumstances outside my control, I found myself feeling pretty desperate.

I've told you the embarrassing story of calling my dad one night to tell him I only had sixteen dollars to my name. It was shortly after the company I'd been working for was shut down unexpectedly, leaving me holding a near-empty bank account instead of the money they owed me. I was in a panic. I had visions of being forced out of my condo, taking the bus everywhere because my car had been repossessed, and sitting on a street corner somewhere playing a guitar, a beat-up suitcase opened in front of me for tips. Worse yet were the headlines I imagined: "NBA Executive's Daughter Found Pan-Handling in Nashville." Oh, the shame of it all.

Anyone who knows me will tell you I am meticulous about my appearance. My idea of "bumming" around on a Saturday afternoon means a full face of makeup and a nice casual outfit, complete with matching shoes, earrings, and hair tie. It's just who I am. One of my splurges has always been getting my nails done. Just like you'll never catch my dad without a book in his hands, well, you'll never catch me without my nails done.

But when I got down to that awful place where I had only a few dollars left to my name, I saw my life in a new light. Maybe I wouldn't be getting my hair done that month. There probably wouldn't be any new clothes for a while. I know it may sound a little trivial, but I'd worked hard to make a living and had grown accustomed to those things, and now they suddenly seemed light-years out of reach.

Now, if there's anyone who can find humor in being virtually broke, it's my dad. When I told him about my financial distress, he "comforted" me with such suggestions as, "Well, you can still get a burger at McDonald's! You can still afford toilet paper at the grocery store! Come on, all is not lost!" In a feeble attempt to match his humor, I blurted out, "Dad, I'm so broke I can't even get my nails done!"

"Hey!" Dad laughed. "That'll be the title of your autobiography after you become a famous musician!" Looking back, I can see how momentary and humorous it all must have seemed to him, but I was not laughing. "Daaaad!" I wailed. "It's not funny!"

This story might lead you to conclude that I haven't done very well following my dad's wise fiscal advice. But we never know when life is going to throw us a curveball like the one that had crossed the plate right in the middle of my personal strike zone. I eventually got

Tithe 10%, save 10%!

through that rough patch and dug out of that financial mess, but it took quite a bit of time and effort—not to mention a few more moments picturing myself on that street corner with my guitar.

Money is a tough area for a lot of people. As soon as that paycheck comes, we feel "rich" for the moment and begin thinking of all the things we want and how that paycheck can get them for us.

Many of my brothers and sisters have struggled in this area as well. All except one, that is. He's the one who was listening to Dad.

I have the greatest big brother in the world. Okay, I'm a little biased. But seriously, Jimmy is the kind of guy to whom people are naturally drawn. Everywhere he goes and in every situation he walks into, people immediately warm up to him.

In the summer of 2007, Jimmy and I were able to spend a few days together in Napa Valley, California, and it was a trip I'll never forget, for it was in those moments that I realized what a lucky "little sis" I am. We laughed and talked for hours. I remember telling Dad when I got home, "I think Jimmy

Williams is the greatest person I've ever known!" Okay, enough of that. He's still my big brother, after all.

When Jimmy was in the eighth grade at Orangewood Christian School in Orlando, one of his classmates was a boy named Tim Seneff, whose dad, Jim, was founder of CNL, a large financial institution in Orlando. One day that year, Jim came in to speak to the eighth graders. His message to those young students was loud and clear: "Don't spend any money until you're thirty!" Advising the class to save instead of spend, Jim went on to explain the progressive advantages of compound interest. He quoted Albert Einstein, who said years ago, "The eighth wonder of the world is the miracle of compound interest."

For some reason, Jimmy was paying attention that day and took in every piece of advice that Jim Seneff offered. I've always suspected Jimmy had inherited an extra dose of the Pat Williams practicality gene, but whatever made it happen, he came home and cooked up a partnership with Granny Williams, Dad's mom. I remember having the distinct impression that Granny was the financial partner and Jimmy the adviser.

I don't know his net worth, but let's just say that at thirty-five Jimmy lives a little differently than the rest of us. It's Jimmy's world, and we're all just visiting. His job in the sports hospitality industry allows him to travel all over the world. He's gotten used to us substituting a game of "Where's Waldo?" with "Where's Jimmy?" when we talk about what he's up to. He has literally been to every country in the world (most more than once). On any given day, you can call Jimmy's cell phone and he'll answer, "Hey, I'm in Thailand, can I call you back?" or "Hey, I'm in the U.K., I'll have to call you back." During holidays, we never know until the day before (or sometimes the day of!) whether or not he's going to show up.

He definitely steps to the beat of a different drummer than the rest of the Williams kids.

Dad began preaching Jim Seneff's advice when I was a teenager. "Don't spend any money until you're thirty." Although I didn't "catch the vision" nearly as young as Jimmy did, and can't say I was wise or self-controlled enough not to spend any money before the age of thirty, I am now allowing the miracle of compound interest to work for me and have made more conscious decisions when it comes to the way I spend my money. It really is a good idea—and here's why.

> *The eighth wonder of the world is the miracle of compound interest.*
> —Albert Einstein

It's so easy to rack up thousands of dollars in credit card debt quicker than you can say "ka-ching"—and then what happens when we hit our max? We go get another credit card. That's brilliant! Sadly, it's also understandable given our current culture of indulgence. But the fact that it's understandable doesn't make it the wise thing to do.

Everywhere we go, the lure to acquire is calling our names. *We want it! We've got to have it!* I've often thought that line in the Lord's Prayer, "lead me not into temptation," has an obvious subtext that reads, "I can find it just fine on my own!"

But if we'll discipline ourselves to put just a little money aside on a regular basis, the miracle of compound interest kicks in, and we'll find in a few years that we actually have that nest egg after all. Here's how Erin Burt explains this "miracle" in the article "Behold the Miracle of Compounding" on Kiplinger.com (http://www.kiplinger.com/columns/starting/archive/2007/st 1107.htm):

> [Compound interest] magically turns a little bit of money, invested wisely, into a whole lot of cash. Even Albert Einstein— a bit of a smarty pants—is said to have called it one of the greatest mathematical concepts of our time.
>
> But you don't need to be a genius to harness the power of compounding. Even the most average of Joes can use it to make money. Trust me. This is so much easier than the theory of relativity.
>
> Here's the gist: When you save or invest, your money earns interest or appreciates. The next year, you earn interest on your original money and the interest from the first year. In the third year, you earn interest on your original money and the interest from the first two years. And so on. It's like a snowball—roll it down a snowy hill and it'll build on itself to get bigger and bigger. Before you know it . . . avalanche!

Now here's the best part: the younger you are when you start exercising this principle, the better it works. So before you rush out to be first on your block with the next-generation techno-gadget, think about whether or not you couldn't put just a little of that paycheck into an interest-earning savings account—and then leave it alone and let it grow. Yes, I wish I'd gotten this idea way back when Jimmy did. But it's better to be a little late than never. So don't worry if you're not yet thirty and you've already spent some money—at least you now have that lesson, too.

I've heard it said that life is often what happens to you while you're making other plans—and I can offer my personal testimony. On my way to Nashville, I was distracted many times before I hit my ultimate stride. Should I go into broadcast journalism, or should I go through that open door to a real estate career? I could see a pretty big pot at the end of that real estate rainbow—so I went that way for a while. Real estate can be very lucrative, a perk I certainly was enjoying. I did my best to follow big brother Jimmy's lead and opened up a few investment accounts. But as the market changed, I felt my heart begin to change as well. I reconnected with my roots and realized how much I missed doing what I really loved. That's when my heart led me to Nashville. Because of the financial tailspin I'd been sent into when the company I worked for closed, my first few months in Nashville were the toughest season I'd ever experienced. But I learned a very valuable lesson from it all as I found myself saying over and over, "I've never been more broke, but

I've never been more fulfilled." There are worse things than having only sixteen dollars in your bank account—but I don't recommend it if you can avoid it!

It's not hard to make tons of money at a job you hate going to every day. Those nice, fat paydays can make it seem worthwhile, materially speaking. And then there are other jobs—jobs that may pay a little less, but are much more fulfilling. Those are the jobs that whisper to your heart, "This is what I was made to do." When I took a job at a publishing house in Nashville, the pay wasn't exactly what I was making in that real estate job. Okay, let's be honest and say it wasn't even close! Because of what I'd been earning previously, I initially considered the offer something of an insult. Dad helped me see the job as a stepping-stone—a great opportunity from which other opportunities would open up. He's good at that. He encouraged me to look at the job—a position I'd likely enjoy even though it wasn't as financially fulfilling—as an "investment" in my future.

The lessons I've learned from my dad over the years often dovetail, and this one is no exception. We need to be wise with our finances and learn about that miracle of compound interest as young as we can, like Jimmy did. But even if we miss it in junior high, there is still time. I'm finally getting it, and I encourage you to get it, too. At the end of the day, however, what matters most is finding a way to get paid for doing what you love. When you spend your time on Earth doing what God put you here to do, you'll be making the best investment of all.

Pat's Lesson

I chuckled when Karyn told the story about Jimmy, Jim Seneff, and my mother. It made me think back to the years I spent growing up in Wilmington, Delaware.

My parents were not advocates of allowances. We never got one. Instead, they encouraged me to get a job. So in sixth grade, at age eleven, I had a morning paper route. I had that route into my senior year in high school. Over the years it grew and became a mammoth task until, after a while, my dad felt sorry for me. He got up and provided the driving while I threw the papers. But anything I wanted to do financially, I had to depend on my own resources.

A big part of my fiscal training came from my mother, who was always teaching me about putting money away. I can still remember my savings book, making deposits, and watching interest accrue. My mother was Jim Seneff before her time! Back in the '50s, she was instructing me in the art of not blowing my money, but putting it away where it could grow. I would buy baseball cards—I admit I was a baseball fanatic and I loved those bubble gum cards—but that paper route money was primarily being stashed away and its interest compounding.

Many years later, I was speaking at an event for CNL Financial Group, Inc., in Orlando, the Jim Seneff–owned company Karyn mentioned earlier. That company, by the way, was started in the Seneff kitchen and is now a world-wide conglomerate. I asked one of the CNL people how they accounted for this growth, and they said, "Compound interest. Jim keeps investing in his company and it just keeps multiplying."

I thought about this in light of a human life. I'm doing things today I could never have done years ago. That's because everything I was doing—investing in my education, my reading, my fitness, my career, my family—all of that investment in years past is now multiplying as I get older. It's compounding. So this principle of compound interest goes beyond dollars and cents. I think it goes into human lives as well. No wonder Einstein called it the eighth wonder of the world.

By the way, the best investment you have is yourself. There's nothing wrong with investing in others—we all need to do that. But you can't be of any use to anybody unless you're investing in yourself. I urge you to (1) invest in the financial area of your life; (2) invest in the family area of your life; and (3) invest in yourself—your ongoing education and your health, your physical fitness. You are the CEO of Yourself.com. If you're going to be able to help *anyone* else, you've first got to be growing and investing in yourself.

Take a lesson from the events on the world scene today, at least here in America. In recent months we've been bombarded by stories about people defaulting on home loans or companies needing to be bailed out. As the post–World War II baby boomers are reaching retirement age, it's becoming painfully evident to many of them that they failed to listen to Mom and Dad's advice way back when. Their failure to save at a time when interest on that money could have compounded is keeping many of them working way beyond traditional retirement age. Don't let this be a lesson you learn too late.

I know it can be tough when there are so many worthwhile goodies to be had in every mall and online store. They may even be calling you specifically by name. But consider those things you just had to have a year ago. Where are they now? What do they mean to you today? I urge you to do whatever it takes to experience the miracle of compound interest in your own life.

THE TAKEAWAY

Don't be so hasty to spend every penny you make before it burns a hole in your pocket.

Save a little from every paycheck and you'll be amazed at how quickly it grows.

As much as you can, resist the temptation and . . .

Don't spend any money until you're thirty!

CHAPTER 15

Choose Your Friends Carefully— Who You Hang with Is Who You'll Become

Y ou probably looked at the title of this chapter, and thought "cliché!" You may have even heard your mom's voice saying, for the quintillionth time, "If all your friends were jumping off the Empire State Building, would you?" We've all heard this piece of advice before, but it was important for me to include this chapter, and I'd like to put a different spin on it for you.

I used to get so frustrated with my dad over this topic. It seemed he was never "impressed" with my friends. I'd introduce Dad to a guy I was dating, and then later ask, "So, what'd you think?" expecting him to validate my eager feelings. Every time, his answer was the same, "Nice guy, nothing wrong with him—but he's a lawn mower."

A lawn mower? How did my dad know in one meeting what the guy did for a living? And why in the world did he care?

But one day, Dad sat me down and explained, "Walt Disney used to say there are three kinds of people in this world, Karyn:

Well Poisoners, Lawn Mowers, and Life Enhancers. Hang with the Life Enhancers."

Noting the question mark on my face, he continued, "Well Poisoners are bad news. If there's an opportunity to rain on your parade, they'll have their galoshes on, ready to induce the downpour. They're the people who have something negative to say about everything. There's no joy in their lives or in their words. They're miserable inside, and they want you to be miserable, too. These people only get pleasure from tearing others down."

Well, that made sense to me. Obviously, I didn't want to hang with those people. In fact, as Dad spoke I reflected on the fact that I'd even cut a few Well Poisoners out of my life already. I was feeling pretty proud about that.

"The Life Enhancers," Dad continued, moving in for the contrast, "are the people who build you up. Everyone loves being around Life Enhancers, and you know it when you're with one. They glow, they smile, they laugh—there's a joy that comes from within. They're quick to hand out compliments because they're secure in themselves. These are the people who are always feeding into your life, investing something of themselves in you. They could not be more unlike the Well Poisoners. You feel good when you hang with Life Enhancers."

Okay, that all made perfect sense. I *don't* want to hang with negative people . . . I *do* want to hang with positive people. Duh! So who were these "Lawn Mower" people?

"The Lawn Mowers," Dad went on, "are tricky. They're the people who get up every morning, get their mower out, and mow their lawn. They work to maintain their lawn, trimming and mowing only what's required on their side of the fence—nothing more, nothing less. They don't bother their neighbors. They're living their lives, doing only what needs to be done, and leaving everything and everyone else alone. They're perfectly happy with the status quo."

Okay, I thought, *but what's wrong with that?* "Are you calling all my friends Lawn Mowers because they wake up every day, work their job, go home at night, eat dinner with their families, and hang out with their friends on the weekends?" I challenged. "Come on, Dad, what's so bad about that?"

Dad wanted me to see that while there was nothing "wrong" with the Lawn Mowers in my life, they weren't people who would enhance my life. He was encouraging me to hang with people who were going to push me to the next level.

The great philosopher Voltaire once said, "The enemy of the best is the good." When I let that statement sink into my brain, it helped me to think differently about a lot of things. So many times we defend things in our life by saying, "It's good! What's wrong with it?" And in truth *nothing* is wrong with it. But maybe the good is causing you to miss out on what is better. Don't let the good rob you of the best.

Surround yourself with life enhancers!

One of my friends confided in me recently about his struggle to get out of a long-term relationship that had run its course and was not really going anywhere. He knew it wasn't right for him anymore. He desperately wanted the joy he saw reflected in other people's relationships, but somehow he kept coming back to this one. I told him, "If you always do what you've always done, you'll always get what you've always gotten."

I once broke up with a guy for this very reason. There was absolutely nothing wrong with our relationship. It was "good." It really was! But somewhere along the line, something began stirring inside me. One day Dad said, "Twenty years from now, you won't be happy with him." Dad was right. It's not that this man was a Well Poisoner, pulling me down in any way—he just wasn't a Life Enhancer, challenging me to get to the next level. Life with him was "status quo," and I knew I could only take so much of that. He was what Dad would call a Lawn Mower.

When I was seven years old, soon after we moved to Orlando, we saw an ad in the *Orlando Sentinel* for those tryouts at Walt Disney World that I mentioned in Chapter 4. The audition for that holiday show was an experience I'll never forget. Every girl I saw waiting to strut her stuff was dressed to the nines in custom-made dance outfits, with hair teased and sprayed so big you could stand in a wind tunnel and it wouldn't move (it was the '80s, after all). Everywhere I looked, I saw moms fussing over the last detail of their daughter's eyeliner, lipstick, or blush. And these girls weren't even out of elementary school!

I, on the other hand, was dressed in a plain purple leotard with my hair in pigtails.

When we walked in and saw the commotion, my mother panicked and immediately thought, *What have I done to my daughter? I'm going to scar her for life!*

But I walked into the audition and stood before the judges. They chatted with me for a minute and then gave me a song to sing with a few simple dance steps. I followed their instructions the best I could and left the room.

A few hours later, when they announced the winners, I don't know who was more shocked by the outcome—the froufrou girls and their moms or me in my plain purple leotard and pigtails, for I had won the part.

Being a part of that show meant I got to perform with Carol Lawrence. Of course, I was too young then to realize that she was a legendary Broadway star and the first woman ever to play the part of Maria in *West Side Story*. I had no idea the impact this woman would have on my life.

The enemy of the best is the good.

I vividly remember meeting her when we walked into one of the halls on the Disney back lot for our first rehearsal. This woman was an absolute delight right from the beginning. Gracious, dignified, polished. She was patient with me as I learned the show; she was generous and kind with her time, and she was so encouraging to me.

As it turned out, my involvement with this show encompassed five years of my life and allowed me to develop a friendship with Carol that continues to this day. I have encouraging handwritten notes from her, and special gifts she gave me along the way that I've treasured over the years. Carol Lawrence is a Life Enhancer to everyone she meets.

Another person who's fed into my life is Kim Boyce (not the Christian singer) with the Fellowship of Christian Athletes (FCA). In high school I did an internship at their office in Orlando under Kim. Part of the program was a once-a-week discipleship time. Kim has enhanced my life in ways even she doesn't realize. She is a faithful friend who has walked with me through many phases of my life. She has prayed with me, laughed with me, cried with me, encouraged me—and literally challenged me to take my life to another level. Like Carol Lawrence, Kim and I remain friends today.

Whether you're five or eighty-five, this rule applies. When you hang with positive, upbeat people, you'll soon become just like them. If you get around a bunch of professional lemon tasters, you'll find your face puckering up so fast you won't recognize your own reflection. There are *no* exceptions.

Picture two people climbing a mountain. Laws of gravity prove it's easier for the guy below to drag his friend down than it is for the guy above to lift his friend up. The Bible even confirms this when it tells us not to be unequally yoked (2 Corinthians 6:14). Paul was speaking to people who were farmers, and they understood that if you hung a yoke over one ox that was strong and another that was weak, the strong ox could not make the weak ox stronger, but the weak ox could pull the strong ox down. It's a life principle.

You're only going to rise as high as the people around you, so surround yourself with people who challenge you. If you're a professional athlete, you wouldn't scrimmage against people you could beat every day, would you? No! If you're going to improve your game, you've got to compete against those who are equal to or even better than you. If you want to obtain better things in your personal and business life, surround yourself with people who have already hit the mark you're aiming for.

Unfortunately, some people are just plain satisfied with the status quo. The only thing they see is the very next step they're going to take and nothing else. They have no vision for where they want to go in the future, and no plan for getting there.

I've done my share of things I'm not proud of, and because of my strong feelings about personal responsibility, I would never place blame on anyone else. But it's clear that many of my regrettable outcomes began with poor choices about the people with whom I chose to spend time.

Not long ago my Nashville pastor, David Foster (not the music producer), said something I found explosive. "When you accumulate the weight of a thousand tiny compromises, you will do things you never thought you would." I thought back over my life and realized that he is right. All of my "big" mistakes began just as he said—with one small compromise, followed by another, then another, and another.

Have you ever really stopped to think about how an affair starts? No one wakes up and says, "I think I'll go start an affair today, *ruin* my marriage, hurt everyone involved, and end up divorced." No, that's not how it works. It starts with the people you surround yourself with. It's a flirtatious comment here and there, spending a little more time together, and one small compromise leads to another. You keep pushing the boundary by saying, "We're just friends. I won't let it get to _____" (fill in the blank with whatever you want), and you find yourself justifying thousands of small compromises. Before you know it, the lives of everyone involved are permanently altered. And it all began by spending a little time with the "wrong" people—people who will bring you down. I have had friends say, "I never thought it would happen to *me*." For some reason, we all think we're immune, and then we're confused when we find ourselves wrapped up in something we don't like. But a thousand small compromises will open the door to places you never wanted to go.

Apply it to whatever you want—drinking, drugs, gambling, overeating, or laziness. It's important to know our own weaknesses and then avoid associating with people who only help us make excuses for ourselves. I heard once that in any given business there are usually only one or two people who would actually steal from their employer. Those one or two will actually scope out the weak people around them, those they can entice into their plans. Don't get roped in. Know your weaknesses and know your strengths. Surround yourself with people who help you play up your strengths.

We talked a lot about this earlier, in our chapter on making good decisions, so I'm not trying to belabor the point, but you and I both know that peer pressure is alive and well. And trust me, it doesn't end after you get out of high school or college. In fact, in some ways, peer pressure can be worse as an adult. You find yourself compromising certain behaviors to impress your new coworkers in order to fit in, or your boss in order to gain that promotion. Surround yourself with the right kinds of people—people who won't lead you into temptation that you can find easily enough on your own, but people who'll help steer you away from it because they know it can hurt you.

If you're feeling pressure from your friends to do things you're uncomfortable with, it's wise to take a second look. Keep in mind that most of the people you're hanging with in high school won't be in your inner circle four years from now. The same goes for college and for "real life." Think about this for a minute: if your friends are pressuring you one way or another— are they really your friends? Look at the people around you now and ask yourself if you like what you see—because who you're hanging with today is who you'll become. Please don't neglect this issue in your life. If you choose to make some changes about who you're "hanging" with, I'll go ahead and warn you that you will catch some heat from your friends when you start to back away. Jealousy comes into play anytime one person is bold enough to try and make a change in his or her life. You may be accused of being "too good" to hang out with your old friends. Expect it. But know it's only jealousy talking, because you've made a decision to improve your life.

The author of the book of Hebrews wrote, "Let us strip off every weight that slows us down" (Hebrews 12:1). I'm not saying you need to clean out your cell phone contacts, ditch your address book, move across the country, and make all new friends, but I *am* challenging you to take an honest look at who you're surrounding yourself with and to ask yourself, honestly, if you're making the best choices.

As for me, I've taken Dad's advice, both about surrounding myself with the right kinds of people and focusing on the Life Enhancers. I hope you will, too.

Pat's Lesson

Every time one of my children has gotten into trouble, I can always trace it back to who they are hanging with, without exception. I mentioned Alan earlier. Alan got hooked up in his junior and senior year with a kid at school who was such a negative influence that Alan couldn't fight it off. As a result, we grounded him for two years. It's in the *Guinness Book of World Records*—look it up! It was the longest grounding in history. Alan gave up being a Magic ball boy, he gave up a driver's license, he gave up *everything* to hang with this kid. That's the power of associations. It goes for adults as well. Whether you're five or eighty-five, the people you hang with are who you're going to become.

I was fortunate early in my sports career to have an association with an important mentor in my life. His name was R. E. Littlejohn, and he was one of the owners of the Spartanburg Phillies baseball club. In February 1965, I became his new twenty-four-year-old general manager. Mr. Littlejohn had a wonderful quality called wisdom. He invested wisdom principles into my life. I've recently written a book called *The Pursuit: Wisdom for the Adventure of Your Life* (Regal Books, 2008), in which I outline six of those wisdom principles that impact me to this day.

1. Control those things over which you have control, and let go of everything else.

2. Be patient.

3. You've got to have experience.

4. Keep it simple.

5. Don't run from your problems; they give you a wonderful chance to sell yourself to others.

6. Pay attention to the little things.

I had great respect for a businessman in the Dallas area named Fred Smith, who died recently at age ninety-two. He had a group of prominent people in his life, including Zig Ziglar—men in their eighties—who still sought him out as a mentor. That's the kind of life I want to lead.

My goal is to be someone people continue to seek out for wisdom, clear up to my dying day. That's one reason why I've always chosen to hang with Life Enhancers. I hope that now that you understand how important this choice is, you will go and do likewise.

THE TAKEAWAY

Take a look at the people in your life and ask yourself, as honestly as you can, if they are Well Poisoners, Lawn Mowers, or Life Enhancers. Then do what you need to do to surround yourself with those who add to your life.

Choose your friends carefully—because who you hang with is who you'll become.

CHAPTER 16

This Is How We Practice Not Quitting

I'll never forget the day my fifty-something dad became a marathon runner. After he finished his first race, I watched him walk through our front door limping, battered, and bruised. He looked like he had been in hand-to-hand combat and was dragging home from the war. I remember thinking, *What in the* world *is fun about that?* But years later when I watched him cross the finish line at the 1997 Chicago Marathon, I caught the bug. Whatever it was that made him want to do this, the satisfaction I saw on his face told me I wanted it, too. So I started training for my first marathon. To date, I've run in nine of these epic events, seven of them right alongside my dad.

One of my favorite memories is of the first time we did the Boston Marathon together. I had trained hard for months, and Dad and I were both pumped. For the first half of the race, I was on fire. I had energy like a madwoman, but Dad was struggling . . . so I did my best to keep him going. Kind of like Frodo and Sam, you know? Though the plan had been to stay

together, he kept saying, "Go! Get a better time if you can . . .
go ahead!" I debated it but decided to stay with him. After mile
thirteen, we stopped for a bathroom break—and I cramped up
really bad. Dad came to life after that, so for the second half
of the race, he had to "carry" me! It was a brutal second half,
and sometime during mile twenty-one, as we were making our
trek up the aptly named "Heartbreak Hill," in agony and
almost in tears, I looked up at Dad and asked, "Why in the
world are we doing this?"

"People ask me that all the time," Dad said, "but you know
why I do marathons? Because this is how I practice not
quitting."

What a *great* perspective. I'll never forget that moment for
as long as I live. I have reminded myself of that statement many
times since that day. I still don't know what's *fun* about
marathons, but I know the immense sense of
satisfaction I feel after running one. It's a
great "I did it!" moment. One more
time, I forced my body to keep going
long past the moment it wanted to quit.

> *The only talent
> is perseverance!*
> —Sally Jesse
> Raphael

I hear people say all the time, "Oh, I
could *never* do a marathon!" And you
know what my response is? "Yes, you could!
Most of it is in your mind." People look at me like I'm crazy, but
trust me, marathons are as much a mental challenge as they are
physical. Basically, from the moment you start, your body wants

to stop. But then your powerful mind kicks in and says, "You started this thing . . . you're *gonna* finish it!" There really is nothing like that feeling—the rush—of knowing you've just beaten those twenty-six miles. The victory is like nothing else.

I've mentioned that my childhood sport was gymnastics. I was obsessed with it morning, noon, and night. Dad drove me to and from practices six times a week. But as I got into middle school, something started to change. I didn't enjoy it as much as I used to. I found myself coming up with excuses for why I couldn't make practices. To this day I don't know what it was that made me lose interest in gymnastics. Maybe it was burnout or maybe it was just developing other interests as I got older. But either way, I quit—cold turkey. My "never quit" dad tried hard to convince me to keep at it, but his stubborn daughter wanted no part of it.

When I made the cheerleading squad in high school, guess what was part of the tryouts? Tumbling! I pulled out some of my old tricks, rusty as they were, but I was sure wishing about then that I had stuck with my gymnastics training. I've often wondered what would have happened if I had made a real commitment to go as far as I could with it. After all, I quit at the age when most elite gymnasts are just beginning to get serious about the Olympics. Could I have done it? I'll never know. I don't beat myself up about it, but it sure taught me a lesson about how quitting may feel "good" for the time being, but it can come back to haunt you.

Rich DeVos, cofounder of the Amway organization, likes to say that perseverance is stubbornness with a purpose. I think that is a terrific quote, and it reminds me that if you quit once, it makes it easier to quit the next time. After you start quitting, it's hard to put the brakes on.

Perseverance is stubbornness with a purpose.
—Rich DeVos

Just before I graduated from high school, I remember asking my dad, "Why'd you let me quit gymnastics?" "*What?*" he said. "*Let* you? Karyn, I pushed, pulled, prodded, begged, and pleaded with you not to quit. But you wouldn't listen." We got a good laugh out of it—because we both knew he was right. But I still had many younger siblings who were competitive swimmers, several of whom were in contention for the Junior Olympics. Because of my personal regrets, I wanted to spare my little brothers and sisters that pain. So I said to Dad, "Well, don't let the other kids quit *their* stuff."

Today, whether it's running a marathon with Dad or finding my way in the country music world, I know I may not be the best, but I *can* guarantee you this: I will work the hardest, I will persevere the longest, and I will strive for lasting quality in my field, no matter what.

And for those of you who may be waiting to take my spot—rest assured, I won't quit—not for anything.

Pat's Lesson

Each of my kids tells me they have at least one story about a time he or she wanted to quit an assignment or a sport—but I wouldn't let them. I remember well the day Karyn came home from school and announced to me, "I quit as captain of the cheerleading squad." And it was only halfway through the school year.

"Oh no, you didn't," I said. "You're going to march right back in there tomorrow morning, get back on the team, and finish out your responsibility!" No child of mine would be a quitter—I was determined about that and wanted Karyn to understand this critical lesson.

I'm glad they remember those moments. With nineteen kids, that's a lot of stories—maybe enough for another book!

Seriously, nothing is worse, in my mind, than taking on a task and then walking out on it before you've finished. You disappoint your teammates, you give up on yourself, and worst of all, you're bailing out on something God has given you to do. Even if the assignment isn't what you thought it would be, or the reality is harder than you imagined, even if it seems impossible—don't give up. God has a purpose he wants to accomplish in you through this test. So don't quit!

One of the big dangers I see coming is that if our kids aren't taught that you don't quit, the personal responsibility factor—already pretty low in my estimation—will diminish even more. People today are quitting right and left—walking out on jobs, on marriages, on families, and on their dreams. Believe me when I tell you that quitting is never an option. We may think *It's my choice, and after all, I'm not hurting anyone but myself.* Don't fool yourself—I've seen quitting cause way too much heartache for everyone involved.

Karyn jokes about the day I used that line about how I practice not quitting, and yes, it clearly made an impression on her. But at thirty years of age, she really doesn't understand yet what it means. She's come close when she explains that the moment we start running the marathon our bodies want to stop.

As we get older, our bodies start screaming out to quit this marathon we're all running—the one we call life. Around age forty-five or fifty we begin experiencing little aches and pains and problems. Have you noticed that yet, moms and dads? My daughter thinks it's amazing that her crazy old dad began running marathons in his fifties or that I climbed a mountain for the first time in that same decade of life—but believe me, I saw this coming on! And I knew that if I gave into it, the old body would win. We are inundated day in and day out with infomercials for health products or ads for in-home fitness equipment and pills that promise to turn back the hands of time, but in the end the only thing that keeps you going is determination and hard work—what John Wayne might have called true grit. Trust me on this: I know that if it's to be, it's up to me. And the same is true for you.

I don't know what health challenges you face, but I do know that sitting around feeling sorry for yourself or making excuses for not moving that body is not going to make it better. Maybe you're in great shape, and if so—congratulations! Just realize that your knees can go when you least expect it. Sadly, the human body will not last forever. It's aging from the moment we are born. But the minute we give up— that's the beginning of the end for us.

Has it ever occurred to you that, even though your body is changing on the outside—the hair a little grayer, one or two more wrinkles as of your last birthday, the pounds a little more difficult to get off—you don't feel one minute older on the inside? Internally, you feel the same as you did when you were eighteen, even though your body may be eighty or older. I believe there is a reason for that. It's because our bodies are mortal, but our spirits are eternal. The Bible tells us that God has planted eternity in our hearts. We're not meant to live here forever! In so many ways, that is thrilling news.

In the meantime, while we're living on this planet, we need to take care of what we've been given. There are so many ways to do that. For you it might be taking a walk every day or running like I do. Maybe you like to go to the gym or get into the pool regularly. The point is—you've got to keep on doing something and challenging yourself physically or your body will one day say, "I'm done." I hope that you, my friend, will be around creating *Takeaway* lessons of your own for a very long time. You do that by practicing not quitting!

THE TAKEAWAY

Quitting is the easy way out, and satisfying only for the moment.

Make a choice to stay the course and run across that finish line. I promise the medal will be worth the blood, sweat, and tears!

One of my favorite quotes comes from Sally Jesse Raphael, who said, "The only talent is perseverance." She gets the message:

This is how we practice not quitting!

CHAPTER 17

There Are No Guarantees That You'll Get Along with Your Family

For reasons known only to him, God chose to place me in a family that was quite colorful—literally speaking. When I was a kid, I thought I had the craziest family ever.

I'm an adult now, and well . . . I still think I have the craziest family ever, but I mean that in the most affectionate way. Today, I am thankful for the family I have, but I'll be honest—that wasn't always the case. Growing up, I struggled with questions like, "God, out of *all* the families in the world, why did you have to put me in *this* one?" and "Why couldn't my family just be normal?" I realize that every family has their "issues" but when I was a child, I thought I had been placed in the most absurd family ever. I don't suppose you've ever thought anything like that.

As I've struggled over the years with certain family relationships, I've heard Dad say over and over, "There are no guarantees you'll get along with everyone in your family." He is *so* right. I would add to that—the bigger your family is, and the more personalities you're dealing with, the more likely that statement is true. Let me tell you how it was in the Williams household.

Our family has been featured on everything from NBC to CNN and had write-ups in *Sports Illustrated*, along with every adoption magazine known to man. We'd have been remarkable enough for our size and diversity, but add to that a dad who's a virtual basketball legend and, well, let's just say it was never dull. Because of the large number of children we have, a lot of attention was given to our adoptions. And the more kids we adopted, the more attention we got. But despite the wonderful publicity we received during my growing-up years, let me assure you—we were not the Cleavers, the Huckstables, or Ozzie and Harriet. I'm not even sure we would have polled well against the Simpsons.

We're all adults now, and I absolutely cherish every one of my brothers and sisters, but I am closer to some than others. There are the ones I talk to regularly, while there are some siblings I don't talk to for months. Maybe it's like that in your family, too. This isn't a bad thing; it's just the way it is. It's interesting, though, that when we get together at Thanksgiving and Christmas, it's like we've never been apart.

The point I'm trying to make is that once we get to be adults, there's no guarantee we'll have close relationships with our siblings—or even with our parents. That doesn't mean that we don't always respect our parents and love and care for our family members, but being close friends is not a given. I used to fret over this. It took me a long time to finally realize it's just a fact—and that's okay.

I talked earlier about my beloved little sisters, Sarah and Andrea. I was the big sister to these two little girls, and I was overjoyed the day they joined our family. We were almost inseparable growing up. I don't look at any of my adopted siblings differently, but Sarah and Andrea are truly the closest things I have to biological sisters.

Today, I understand that old Chinese proverb that says, "Nobody's family can hang out the sign, 'Nothing the matter here.'" But as a teenager, I experienced a family problem that devastated me. The day my parents' divorce began, life came to a screeching halt—and my family scattered. We completely fell apart. We were in so much pain that, instinctively, we all just shut down.

Dad did his best to keep our family afloat financially, all the while dealing with an ugly divorce battle and his own emotional pain. All of us kids did our best to put one foot in front of the other every day, but we were dying inside. It was as if all the life in that very lively household had just been sucked out.

For Sarah and Andrea, many years of built-up resentment and jealousy came out during that time. They separated themselves and bonded to one another—and I was the odd sister out. I lost my relationship with them to some degree. We went several years without communicating at all. It felt like someone had taken an ax and chipped off a small piece of me.

A few years later, after Sarah had married and found out she was pregnant with her first child, she began coming around again . . . slowly. Once she had reengaged with the family, Andrea soon followed, making brief appearances every now and then.

Not long after Sarah's baby was on the way, Andrea found out that she, too, would be a mom. Now that they are both parents, their outlook on life is completely different. We've slowly begun to rebuild our relationships. I've felt their hearts soften, and that's led to many, many conversations about "what went wrong." After all the time we lost, whenever we're together I want to soak up every second I can. When I see them with their little girls, it's all I can do not to dissolve in tears. We've walked through the "fire" of our tumultuous past and now share a warm, close, adult friendship.

My sister Daniela was adopted from Brazil when she was eleven years old. Dani, as we call her, was a difficult child. She lived a very hard life during her early years in Brazil, and she was quite the troublemaker when she joined our family. Dani immediately took to Dad, and, to be honest, I struggled with that. He was *my* dad. After our parents broke up, Dani went her own way for a while. She dropped out of school and became a real rebel. Dani and I also went several years without any contact. If someone had wanted to contact her, I couldn't have told them how to get in touch with her. She had literally dropped out of my life, and I had dropped out of hers.

Like that lost son the Bible talks about in Luke 19, after a few years of reality, Dani made a major turnaround and eventually came back into the fold. She finished high school, started college, and is now on her way to a degree at the University of Central Florida. She's even talking about getting a master's degree, and she is the pride and joy of our family. It's been remarkable to watch the transformation in this young woman who has seen more in her lifetime than I could even begin to imagine. And where once I had no relationship with her, today she's the first person I'm dying to see every time I visit Orlando.

One of the most meaningful things I own is a scrapbook Dani made for me when I moved from Orlando to Nashville. I remember that on the morning I left, I stopped by for one more hug from Dad. There was Dani, and she came running up to me with her arms flailing. "Karyn, wait! I have something for you!" She left for a minute and came back carrying the most beautiful scrapbook I've ever seen. She'd made it herself, using recent photos of all of us kids. It was all I needed to send me over the edge emotionally one more time. I opened the scrapbook and felt the lump in my throat rise again. As I flipped through the pages, Dad looked over my shoulder, and we reminisced about the last few years with my brothers and sisters.

I really can't describe what I felt in those moments. They were so bittersweet. On the one hand, I was overwhelmed to be standing there with my sister, an incredible woman with whom I had walked a tough road. I was excited about the journey I was about to embark on, but on the other hand, I was devastated to be moving away from home when things had just gotten "good" with Dani and me. I joked with God, saying, "Why do I have to leave home now when my family has finally been put back together?"

I flipped to the last page and saw a picture of all of us together. Dani had handwritten the message: *You'll always know where home is.*

Nothing could have prepared me for that.

I tell you these stories simply to show you that no family is perfect. Mine is certainly no exception. The Williams kids have seen years of great fun and laughter. But we've also experienced the shattering of relationships that took many years and many tears to put back together. During those rough years, I thought all was lost. I felt hopeless and helpless. I could *never* have imagined the healing that has now taken place.

Reconciliation is always the best path to choose, but I won't kid you—it is not an easy one to travel at first.

There is no point in playing the blame game!

I guarantee that back in the day, if you had picked up a magazine or caught a news story on our family, you would have thought we were the epitome of happiness. Whenever the cameras came around, we all put our best smiles on. We became masters at "faking it." This actually caused me to develop a few bad habits relationally. I had to unlearn them and realize it's okay to show my feelings in appropriate ways and times. Because of those experiences, whenever I see smiling photos of celebrity families, I silently say a prayer that it's really the case.

Families are complicated. Every family deals with jealousy, anger, and lies, and sweeping things under the rug for the sake of "image." Even Dad and I, close as we are, have struggled from time to time in our relationship. Usually it was over something I wanted to do with my life that he didn't agree with, which frustrated me to no end. Can you relate? Since this book is built around his advice, I am here to say that he was and still is usually right—but I can't deny there have been times in my life when I'm glad I followed my own lead. *If I had listened to Dad*, I remember thinking, *then I never would have transferred from Indiana University to the University of Florida, which means I never would have entered the Miss University of Florida pageant, which means I never would have entered Miss Florida, which means I never would have gone to Nashville to begin with.* That doesn't make it right or wrong; it's just the way it is. At the end of every "what should I do with my life" discussion, Dad always says the same thing. "It's your life Karyn. These are your decisions to make." And I try to remember that golden advice about the wise thing to do. No matter what safeguards we build into our lives, we will all screw up from time to time. What matters is realizing God has our lives in his control. It does no good to blame anyone else for what could or could not have happened.

I know so many people who continually beat themselves up because of failed family relationships. I'm not saying to give up on those relationships, but please don't spend years beating yourself up. Keep praying for them and loving them. You never know when things may turn around. But you can't control what goes on in someone else's heart.

I used to go to the restaurant where my sisters worked in Orlando and they would literally act like they didn't know me. It was devastating. But your life is your own, and it's up to you to decide in your heart that one day things *will* turn around. The Bible says we should be "quick to listen, slow to speak, and slow to anger" (James 1:19). Swallow your pride and apologize for whatever part you may have played in the breakdown of the relationship. Pointing fingers and blaming everything in sight isn't going to do any good. Just face it head-on.

There are some family relationships where *you* may be the one keeping others at arm's length for any number of reasons. Maybe it's your mother who has hurt you with words over and over and you've decided to end the cycle. Maybe it's been years of sexual abuse by your grandfather and it's too difficult to have a relationship. There are relationships that can be destructive, and sometimes the best thing to do is to remove yourself. I love how Naomi Judd put it when she said, "You're only a victim once. After that, you're a volunteer."

You may have a family relationship so unhealthy you've decided to end it. First, let me say that that is a decision only you can make. Everyone you know will have an opinion about it, but only you can decide what's emotionally healthy for your own life. I'm not advocating burning family bridges here; I'm simply saying that it's okay if you've chosen to remove yourself from a damaging relationship. You may be in a hopeless place right now, wondering how in the world things have turned out as they have. You may think you're destined to have bad family relationships, or you feel like everything is your fault—and by the way, it is not. Please remember, you can't control anyone but yourself.

> *You can't control what goes on in someone else's heart.*

There is one particular relationship in my life that has never been easy—I've struggled with it for as long as I can remember. I made a decision to walk away from it for many years and caught a lot of heat for it, but I knew it was the healthiest thing for me at the time. Many years later, I was finally able to enter back into the relationship, now with the proper boundaries I could live within.

If you're experiencing something like this right now, please let me encourage you by saying that you're *not* destined to a lifetime of guilt and pain. In the relationship I mentioned above, I struggled with feelings of, "Why does this have to happen to me? What did I do to deserve this?" But in reality, there are thousands of people dealing with similar situations. Lots of people have a difficult family member. The beautiful thing is that God knows exactly what we're going through and exactly what we need. He wants to fill the voids in our lives. To that end, he may give you a wonderful stepmom, or bring a wonderful father figure into your life, or wonderful girlfriends that will "substitute" as sisters. He can take what we see as devastating and turn it into something beautiful. Is it the same? No. Is it easy? Not always. But he hears your cries, knows your needs, and wants to fulfill every desire in your heart—including restored family relationships.

Interestingly enough, as I was writing this chapter, I received a package in the mail. It was a used book I had ordered from Amazon.com. When I opened the book, a piece of paper fell out, so I picked it up. It was a handwritten note that had been tucked inside the book, to a girl named Michelle. This is what it said:

Michelle,

I am sorry that you think we don't care about you and your life. We do! You are our child—we will always care. We love you! Please don't forget that. I hope you have a wonderful day tomorrow. Remember, before the earth was formed, God had a plan for your life. Trust him.

Love, Mom

I have no idea who Michelle is, nor do I know anything about her relationship with her mom. But I have no doubt someone there was hurting. What an amazing note of affirmation to have come in the mail just as I was writing about difficult family relationships.

When it's all said and done, our family is sometimes all we've got. Unfortunately, so many people are hurting and wanting to rebuild lost relationships. Please don't give up hope. Let the stories of my renewed relationships and reset boundaries encourage you that all is not lost, and that the Lord can soften hearts that have been hurt. As Michelle's mom said in her note, trust him.

Pat's Lesson

Family problems are as old as Cain and Abel—and we all know how that turned out. Even President Harry S. Truman knew what that difficulty was like. He once said, "I had numerous aunts and uncles and some thirty cousins. These kinfolk were all on good terms with me, but hardly ever with one another. It was my duty to be the family peacemaker." Over the years, I've learned Truman's secret: family problems don't have to be as deadly as Cain's and Abel's if we'll simply soften our hearts toward one another.

Most family problems begin with hardened hearts and people unwilling to forgive. I've seen that in own family. Years ago, my younger sister, Ruth, my mother, and my family bought a cottage at a wonderful mountain resort in Pennsylvania called Eagles Mere. We'd spent summers there as kids, so when this cottage became available, we couldn't resist it. The three of us purchased it together, planning to split the time over the course of the year.

It turned out to be a disaster. We really could not agree on much of anything. My sister, Ruth, and I, who had been very close, went *eight years* without speaking as a result of this cottage fiasco. Finally, we broke the ice, asked for forgiveness over the whole incident, healed our relationship, and now are closer than ever.

In a family as large as ours, it would take an MIT mathematician to figure out all the dynamics possible with so many human beings. The children have gone through periods of noncommunication and distance from each other, but I've also seen them come back around. I can tell you firsthand, it only happened when they were willing to forgive.

Perhaps you have gone through experiences similar to this. All I can tell you is that life is very short. In fact, I've observed that life is like a roll of toilet paper. The closer you get to the end, the faster it goes. We do not know what tomorrow holds for any of us, so if there are any breaks or separations in your family relationships, get them straightened out, resolve them now, and seek to live in peace and harmony. While you're doing it, remember the cottage in Eagles Mere. I heard this quote somewhere, and while I don't know where it originated, it's one with which I could not agree more: "To forgive is to set a prisoner free—and to discover that the prisoner was me." Forgiveness is the only sure path to healing broken relationships.

THE TAKEAWAY

*God never said we had to like our family mem-
bers, but we do have to love them.*

*Do what you need to do for yourself, trust God
with the details, and watch him do the impossible.
In the meantime, realize that . . .*

**There are no guarantees that you'll
get along with your family.**

Chapter 18

Does He/She Make You a Better Person?

I was one of those hardheaded kids who had to screw up a lot on my own before the truth would sink in. Ever know anyone like that? Now that I'm an adult, I finally realize that 99.9 percent of the time, my parents are right. Of course, it helps to know they are both continually in God's Word, so I am reassured they're not relying simply on their own wisdom. But in my own not-so-unique style, I had to learn this truth the hard way.

When I was nineteen and a contestant for Miss Florida, I met a young man I was convinced was Mr. Right. Boy, was I taken with him! He was good-looking, charming, funny, and smart. He even had a good job. He was everything I had ever dreamed of—a genuine Prince Charming. We began dating and it got serious quickly. I was in love and everything was right in my world. Everything except one, that is. Dad wasn't happy.

I had one more year left at the University of Florida before I would graduate and had just won first runner-up in the Miss Florida pageant. If I decided to go back the next year, there was a good chance I would win and then head to Atlantic City to compete for the coveted title of Miss America. But Mr. Right wanted to get married. What was I to do? I didn't want to disappoint Mr. Right. After all, we were in love. That's all you need to get married, right?

Now, Dad *really* wasn't happy. "Karyn, you aren't finished with school yet," he argued, "and you have to make a run at Miss America next year!"

This was not what I wanted to hear. Not only was I ready to walk down the aisle—right now—but that negative pageant experience I mentioned in Chapter 12 had soured me on the contest. In that moment, I didn't want any part of it. So, Mr. Right and I continued our relationship, along with the wedding plans. Deep inside, I knew Dad was right. I just didn't want to admit it. I wanted what I wanted.

That fall, instead of going back to school, I headed to Nashville to record my first demo album. In my mind, I was on my way to a career in music. But the opportunity didn't agree. Before I knew it, I was back in Orlando waiting tables—and dating Mr. Right again.

I knew he wasn't a committed Christian, and I'd been taught all my life to make sure this spiritual connection was there. As I mentioned in Chapter 15, the Bible warns us not to be unequally yoked. But he was such a good guy! Surely he'd change after we were married, wouldn't he? But he *had* gone to church throughout his life. Wasn't that close enough? But, Dad didn't like it.

One day someone I knew and trusted asked him, "Why would God let you into heaven?" And I cringed inside as I heard Mr. Right say, "Because I'm a good person and I've lived a good life." Oh, I *knew* that was the wrong answer! You'd think that would have set off a five-alarm warning bell. But love, as they say, is blind. Not to mention stubborn.

At Dad's insistence, we went through Christian counseling and a premarital class at my church. In addition, Dad mercilessly grilled Mr. Right to pieces, all the while doing everything he could to change my mind. But remember, I thought I had all the answers.

Trust your gut instinct!

In the end, Dad's desperate measures didn't work. Reluctantly, he finally agreed to walk me down the aisle. In December 2001, with all the warning flags flying at full mast, I married Mr. Right.

It was a fairy-tale wedding. Who could have guessed how quickly it would turn into a horror story? The twist occurred on our honeymoon. It was one of those stories you read about happening to other people—not to anyone you know and especially not to you. Even though we had dated for two years before we got married, it wasn't until after the wedding that I got to know the "real" person I was dealing with. Overnight, Mr. Right turned into Mr. Oh-So-Wrong.

Now I may be stubborn, but I'm not stupid. Immediately, I knew I had made a huge mistake. But divorce was not an option in my mind. I had worked very hard convincing everyone in my life that this decision was right, and biblically, I knew divorce was never the best decision.

So I threw everything I had into making it work. I didn't tell anyone what was really going on, but I was definitely living with Dr. Jekyll and Mr. Hyde—it was truly a nightmare. In public, I wore my game face. No one must know I was dying inside. I desperately didn't want to be "that" couple—the one always having problems.

Finally, after three-and-a-half years, I cracked. I wasn't ready yet to admit it to Dad, so I went to my "other" rock—my amazing stepmom, Ruth. She listened, stunned, as I told her about the emotional and mental abuse that had been going on behind closed doors. "You've put on a good show, Karyn," she said. And then she quietly coached me through the next three months.

I tried hard, but no matter which solution I tried, nothing worked. When I finally realized I would be facing a divorce, I asked myself which was worse—saying the word or telling Dad. After all, he hadn't wanted me to marry this man in the first place. My heart sank as I recalled the day he told me point-blank, "Karyn, this is *not* the man for you." I hadn't listened. And now I was paying a heavy price.

I had visions of Dad sticking out his tongue, putting his fingers up to his ears, and chanting, "Told ya so, told ya so!"

But he didn't. In fact, when I finally confessed to him, we had one of the tenderest conversations we've ever had. He was as stunned by my admission as Ruth had been. "Karyn," Dad said, "I don't agree with divorce, but I also don't agree with the way you're living. You need to get out of there."

I'm not proud of this piece of my history. I struggled internally a long time with having the "D" word on my résumé. Years later, when one man I went on a date with condemned me for being divorced, I went into an emotional tailspin, convinced no Christian man would ever want me. I saw myself as spoiled goods.

You will be a different person at twenty-five than you are at twenty.

In God's book, however, even bad stories can have happy endings. I can truthfully say that the Lord has turned my poor decision into something beautiful. Because of the trouble I went through, my relationship with God has deepened to a whole new level. During all that awful time of abuse and lies when I was afraid to admit the truth to anyone, I had no one else to lean on but him. And believe me, I leaned!

My experience has also deepened my relationship with my earthly father. Finally sharing my feelings and heartache with Dad made for some long, intense talks—and this time, I was ready to listen. No way was I going to go through an awful nightmare like that again.

The other positive thing that has come from my experience is my desire to share the lessons I've learned with you. If I can spare you from making the same mistake I did, or comfort you with the fact that you are not alone, then it will have been worth the pain.

"Karyn," Dad says now, "before you get married, you need to ask yourself some very simple questions: 'Does he make me a better person? Does he help me become the woman I want to be? And do I do the same for him?'" One of my favorite lines is from a song I cowrote that says, "Does he take your every dream and give you wings?" In my case, the answer was a definite "no" to all of these questions, and when I'm being totally honest with myself, I knew that going in.

If you are in a place like that right now, I urge you to listen to that little voice inside—the one you're trying hard to ignore or deny. Don't turn it off or tell it to go away. Listen to it! Heed the warning call before it's too late. I know you don't want to hear it. But oh, I hope you will.

A Message for
Those Under Twenty-Five

Let me shoot straight with you for just a minute here. I read many books when I was younger that said "Don't get married until you're at least twenty-five." At seventeen, eighteen, nineteen, and even twenty-four—we do *not* want to hear those words. But allow me to save you a lot of heartache and tell you—*they're right*!

We go through so much growth and change during our early twenties. Believe me when I tell you, you will be a different person at twenty-five than you were at twenty. And you'll be a different person at thirty than you were at twenty-five. It is so exciting to experience the growth that takes place when you trust the Lord with your life entirely, not worrying about getting married or depending on someone else. The only way to do that is to simply release it to God. Let him take the controls, follow his lead—and listen to his messengers.

If you've already made the decision to marry and you're not yet twenty-five, please know I am praying for you. The road you are on is a difficult one. But it doesn't mean you are doomed to fail. Hold on to God. It's amazing what we can overcome with his help.

No matter what happens, know that we serve the God of Second Chances. He is in the restoration and renewal business. God has forgiven me for my mistake and has put me back on the road to righteousness. No matter who you are, who you've been hanging with, or where you've been, please know that God is not interested in condemning you for your yesterdays. He is only interested in where you are headed from this moment on.

Today, I recognize my dad as God's messenger in my life. By sharing with you the questions about marriage that he has drilled into my head over the past few years, maybe he can be your messenger, too:

- Does he/she make you a better person?
- Do you make him/her a better person?
- Is this person growing in their faith (on their own, without your prompting)?
- Are you ready to have 15,000 dinners with this person over a period of fifty years?
- Does he/she challenge you physically? Spiritually? Mentally?
- Do you have fun together?
- Can you drive for ten hours on a trip and talk nonstop?
- Does he/she recognize your dreams and give you wings to fly?

If it helps, copy the previous page and put it up on your bathroom mirror. If you find yourself in a relationship in which you don't want to look at these questions, much less answer them, I'm telling you here and now, that relationship spells trouble. Do yourself a lifetime favor and get it right the first time. You have the tools, now *please* put them to use.

Pat's Lesson

Karyn will tell you that I have always viewed life as an adventure.

In early September 1996, I embarked on a wild escapade of trying to climb Mount Rainier. A blizzard kept us from summiting, but boy, I came down from that climb with a *ton* of life lessons. One of them is that in life, we are all climbing a mountain.

I learned on that mountain that it sure helps to have a good climbing partner. That makes the task a lot more efficient. In climbing the mountain of life, if you have the right marriage partner, it makes all the difference in the world. If your marriage partner is trying to pull you off the side of the mountain, or pull you down the mountain, or is lying down and trying to get you to drag them *up* the mountain, that can be exhausting and debilitating, and it will never work. On the other hand, if you have a climbing partner in marriage who is in step with you—or even out front, helping you get to the top of that mountain—what a wonderful blessing that is.

After a difficult first marriage, I remarried in 1997. Ruth has been a wonderful climbing partner. In our life we have *many* trails, and they all lead to magnificent adventures. Ruth is an outstanding author in her own right, and she's a public speaker. Those are two of my fields as well, and she has been infinitely helpful to me in those areas. She has run twelve marathons with me and has helped *immeasurably* in raising nineteen children (and seven grandchildren). She pays the bills, does the laundry, oversees the financial investments, does the taxes, decorates the house, sometimes squeezes in a few hours' sleep, does the grocery shopping, makes the bed—the list goes on and on. And in her spare time, Ruth is studying to get her Ph.D. in organizational leadership!

All she does has allowed me, for the past dozen years or so, to live to my full potential. She's a cheerleader and an encourager, and she never complains. When I have to travel, it's always with her full support. Anyone who's on the road like I am understands it's tough to do if your mate is pulling you in the other direction. I'm living through the experience of being a better person as a result of who I married. I've been on both sides, and I can tell you, this one is better. She truly makes me a better person, and I pray I'm returning the favor.

I originally heard this "better person" philosophy from Mike Krzyzewski, the basketball coach at Duke University. Mike and his wife have three daughters, and when they wanted to get married, Mike simply asked one question: "Does this man you plan to marry make you a better person?"

He asked the same question of the young men: "Does my daughter make you a better person?" It's a great concept— and it works. I hope you will ask yourself that question in your own relationships. By the way, if you're already in a committed relationship and you feel alarmed that perhaps your answers would have been "no," it's not too late to do damage control. One way to repair your situation is by determining that, as far as it's up to you, you will make your mate a better person. When we do that from a genuine servant's heart, it's amazing how often God turns a struggling relationship around. Believe that he can do the unexpected.

THE TAKEAWAY

No matter how hard it might be right now, you've got to ask yourself if the person you're involved with makes you a better person. If the answer is no, decide what to do about it. Get help if you need to. Ask God for strength to walk away if you're not yet married. And if you are, ask him to show you what you can do to make your partner a better person—then watch God surprise you. For now, ask yourself . . .

Does he/she make you a better person?

CHAPTER 19

Be the Woman or Man YOU Want To Be

I've mentioned elsewhere in this book that I have a wonderful relationship with my stepmom, Ruth. In a conversation with her one day, we were discussing Dad's phrase, "Does he make you a better person?" Ruth said something that opened up the meaning of Dad's lesson in a whole new way. Her comment really affected me and has since inspired a beautiful song that has become a personal mantra of mine.

Girls, you know "that list" you wrote when you were in high school, or maybe college, the one that describes your perfect mate? Well, I had a list of my own, and one day I was excitedly talking about a new guy I had been dating and how he met all of the attributes I had written out on my list. It was as if I'd been checking them off, one by one, since our first date. Ruth, in her sweet Southern manner, said, "I know a lot of girls do that, but I don't agree with that list." "Why?" I asked. "Because in that list, you're describing a perfect man, and there is no such thing." Back down, fellas—you know it's true, even if you don't want to admit it.

Ruth continued, "Instead, I think girls should write out a list of qualities they want to have as a wife and then find a partner who brings those qualities out."

"Hmm," I said, and began to process her theory. "So, it's like this—is *he* the man who makes *me* the woman *I* want to be?"

Ruth smiled. "*Exactly.*"

I couldn't get the phrase out of my mind, and not long after that I had a writing appointment with Brian White and Steve Dean, two of my favorite cowriters in Nashville. We were tossing around song ideas that day, and I felt strongly that I needed to throw this idea out there. I thought for sure they would think it was too "girly" and drippy, and we'd continue on to the next idea. But I risked it anyway. They both stopped and looked at each other, then over at me and said, "If we don't write that today, we're crazy!" Now, wherever I sing it, people stop me to comment on what a great message it has.

You decide who you'll become!

We've all struggled with the influences certain people can have in our lives. I'm no exception. I've allowed people to get close who were impacting my life in negative ways, and I've stayed in those relationships longer than I should have. One night when I was still living at home, I went to my dad in a mess of tears and poured out my heavy heart to him. I was feeling trapped and frustrated with who I saw myself becoming based on this harmful influence. Even though I was still fairly young, I remember what my dad said like it was yesterday. After a brief discussion about choosing carefully the people we "hang" with, my dad said, "But Karyn, *no one* can dictate the woman you will turn out to be except for you. *It's your choice.*"

It was as if my heart had been given a new lease on life. In that moment I realized I had been living under a dark cloud, believing I was destined to grow up to be someone I wouldn't like very much. My dad literally changed my life that day with a few wise sentences. I began looking at myself as my own person, someone in total control of her relationship choices. I had not just the freedom, but the responsibility to "hang" with the Life Enhancers we met in Chapter 15. There is something so liberating about realizing you are a uniquely created individual, made by God to be you, and only you.

One dismal day a few years ago, I was struggling with loneliness, thinking perhaps I would never find the right mate. I had broken up with a boyfriend simply for the fact that I just *knew* he wasn't right for me long-term. It was hard. Tears flowing freely down my face, I decided to take a quick shower to distract myself. Maybe that would wash away my sadness. As I dried off, I was overcome with a tremendous urge to open my Bible to the book of James. These words both confronted and comforted me: "Consider it pure joy, my brothers, whenever you face trials of many kinds, because you know that the testing of your faith develops perseverance. Perseverance must finish its work so that you may be mature and complete, not lacking anything" (James 1:2–4). What a powerful promise to a girl who was wondering if she would ever feel "complete."

Just as I was about to close my Bible, I found a piece of paper tucked inside it. When I unfolded it, I remembered putting it there several years before. It was a piece of wisdom someone had handed me. Here is what it said, "You must decide what kind of a person you will love before passion takes over. Determine whether a person's character and faith in God are as desirable as his physical appearance. Because most of the time you spend with your spouse will not involve sex; your companion's personality, temperament, and commitment to solve problems must be as gratifying as his kisses. Be patient. The second look often reveals what is beneath the pleasant appearance and attentive touch."

Needless to say, I was stunned. It was just what I needed to hear that day. But the story gets even better. I turned the paper over and realized I had written the date on the back: "11/2/99." The date on which I had reread the words was 11/2/2006— seven years later to the day. Some people would call that "coincidence," but I don't think it's coincidence at all. I think God "winked" at me that day to gently remind me that he is with me always—on the happy days and the sad, on the days when I feel triumphant, and on those days when it seems like nothing's working and I've wanted to take a long walk off a short plank!

You and I were uniquely created by God, and because of that, there's not another person like us walking on Earth—never has been before, never will be again. He was reminding me in that moment that he knows the exact number of hairs on my head and freckles on my body. He knows my every thought, and he cares about every tiny detail of my life. On the days when I doubt

> *Decide what kind of a person you will love before passion takes over!*

myself, he doesn't doubt me. He gently walks beside me every day as I continually strive to become the best woman, daughter, sister, aunt, friend, and yes, eventually, wife that I can be.

No matter what smorgasbord has been packed into your life, you have that same potential. Just as Dad said to me all those years ago, the same is true for you—you get to choose the person you grow up to be. I read a quote the other day from sixteenth-century author Miguel de Cervantes (*Don Quixote*), who said, "Everyone is as God has made him, and oftentimes a great deal worse." It's a funny statement, but also tragic if we are worse when we could have prevented it. That's why it's so critical, as we've said throughout this book, that you make wise decisions—about your actions, who you hang out with, how you use your leisure time, what you ingest—everything! Who you are is not about who you are with—it's about you and your character and how you treat others and whether or not you're pursuing your dreams. We can get the wrong idea sometimes that who we are is dependent upon having someone in our lives, a significant other—but that's really a choice, too. And it's one we'd better make carefully. We had a saying in our house (I can still hear my big brother Jimmy saying it). It was simply this: YOU are responsible. We're all responsible for our own actions, our own happiness, our own successes and failures. As former first lady Eleanor Roosevelt said, "In the long run, we shape our lives, and we shape ourselves. The process never ends until we die. And the choices we make are ultimately our responsibility."

So when you're making out your own "list," I hope you give a lot of thought to that person you are in continual process of becoming. What qualities are you choosing to build into your one and only life? When it comes to choosing a partner, I hope you'll remember Ruth's question: Does he make you the woman you want to be? Guys, does she make you the man you want to be? If the answer is no—keep looking. You've got all the time in the world.

Pat's Lesson

When it comes to being the best you can be, men tend to think in terms of investment, usually an investment in the business area of their life—investment in the stock market, investment in real estate, investment in growing a company. That's just how we men think. What I've learned over the years—and believe me when I say I have learned it the hard way—is that the best investment a man has is his wife, because everything you invest in her will pay enormous dividends over time. So the greatest advice I can give you, men, is to keep investing in your wife. Now the obvious question is, "Well, how do I do that?"

Years ago while in the midst of a marital crisis, I was introduced to a book called *Love Life for Every Married Couple* (Zondervan, 1980). Its author, Dr. Ed Wheat, was a medical doctor in Springdale, Arkansas. In the course of his medical practice, Dr. Wheat saw women struggling terribly with nonphysical issues. Over time he realized they were depressed and desperately unhappy in their marriages. He investigated further and discovered that eventually, these women would die emotionally. The pilot light within them had completely gone out. When he described husbands who became frantic, I recognized myself and realized my marriage was in deep trouble. Men and women readers, hear me—if your marriage is having problems, you need to know this!

Dr. Wheat had developed an acrostic that gave me a clear picture of what is required to be a good husband. Using the letters B.E.S.T., he laid it all out—a formula designed to revive dead marriages. Before the marriage dies, guys, to help your woman be the woman you want to be with, understand the B.E.S.T. theory:

Blessing: We bless others when we praise them and express gratitude for what they have done for us, or even simply for the fact that they are in our lives.

Edifying: To edify means to build up. We edify our mates by showing them full support, by encouraging them in all they do, and by speaking well of them to others.

Sharing: When we marry, the Bible tells us we become "one flesh," and it's true that our lives are joined in a mysterious way. Everything we are and everything we have is no longer ours alone, but components in a joint partnership in which everything is shared equally. When it comes to communicating our feelings, men, our wives especially want us to share our hearts with them. This does not come naturally, but I'm here to tell you it can be learned.

Touching: In the early stages of our relationships, touching is not the problem—in fact, that stage is frequently marked by *too much* touching. But when troubles arise, we retreat. We back away from the relationship and touching decreases. For there to be true intimacy in our marriages, we've got to understand the vital importance of nonsexual touching.

This amazing advice from Dr. Wheat came into my life at just the right time. Until the day I picked it up, I'd never realized there were foundational principles for successful marriages. We men tend to get caught up in our careers and in the acquiring of things to fill our homes, all too often expecting our wives to just shift into cruise control and come along for the ride.

Let me tell you, friends, as a man who's seen love from all sides, and who's experienced both the difficulties and the joys that marriage has to offer, when you're looking for investments to make for lifelong security, you'll never go wrong investing in your wife.

As I told my little Karyn all those years ago, no one but you can ultimately dictate the person you turn out to be. It's my hope you'll choose to become someone who invests in the lives of others. I don't know any better way to guarantee a happy life for yourself.

THE TAKEAWAY

Never think you are fated to be just like anyone but you. Each one of us is uniquely created.

Our job is to become the person we were born to be.

Who you are is your choice. Do what you must to . . .

Be the woman or man YOU want to be!

CHAPTER 20

Stay Close to the Lord

He Is with You on the Mountain as Well as in the Valley

In spring 2005, I made the toughest decision I've ever had to make. I swallowed my pride and chose to leave an abusive marriage, which meant starting my adult life over. For the first few months, Dad and Ruth graciously allowed me to move back into their home until I got back on my feet. It was comforting to have my family close, but I still had my tough days when the tears flowed all too easily.

One afternoon I was having a particularly tough time. I remember my sweet daddy wrapping me up in his big arms. He held me as I cried and said, "Stay close to the Lord, sweetheart. He's with you on the mountains as well as in the valleys." In that moment, I realized I hadn't been doing that. The Scripture says to "cast your cares upon him, for he cares for you" (1 Peter 5:7), but I hadn't been obedient at all. I'd been holding on to my cares, nursing them for all my might and letting them rule my life. Of course, God wanted me to give them to him. Why had I forgotten how much bigger he is than I am?

That day, Dad reminded me of this important truth. The Lord wants us to depend on him all the time—whether we're on top of the world or sinking into the quicksand faster than our little hands can dig. In Psalm 50, God says, "Call upon me in the day of trouble; I will deliver you, and you will honor me" (Psalm 50:15). In another place, he tells the psalmist, "'Because he loves me,' says the LORD, 'I will rescue him; I will protect him, for he acknowledges my name. He will call upon me, and I will answer him; I will be with him in trouble, I will deliver him and honor him. With long life will I satisfy him and show him my salvation'" (Psalm 91:14–16). And he promises the prophet Jeremiah, "Then you will call upon me and come and pray to me, and I will listen to you" (Jeremiah 29:12). How much clearer could he be? God understands our pain and wants to carry us through it, if we'll just let him.

Let go— and let God do the rest!

As I've mentioned elsewhere, when I was in high school, I watched my parents go through a very painful divorce. It was a season I thought would kill us all. I had no idea that my family was about to fall apart—*big-time*.

There was one night during that rough season when all of us kids were sitting in the living room listening to music when Dad came home from work. I don't remember exactly what we were listening to, but I do know it was a Christian tape or CD. When he walked in the door, I went over and gave him a big hug. He held me for the longest time, and then he started shaking. It took a few seconds for me to realize he was crying. We knew that our mom had moved out and that things were not looking good, but it wasn't until the *Orlando Sentinel* came out the next morning that we realized he had been served with the divorce papers that day. The divorce had officially begun. During one of the hardest times of his life, it overwhelmed him to come home and see all his kids bonded together listening to Christian music.

How could God allow this to happen to me?

I admit that I struggled with my faith a bit during that tough time. Where was God in all of this? How could he allow this to happen to our family? Why couldn't our house just be a peaceful place instead of what felt like a war zone?

We owned a condo in New Smyrna Beach, Florida, during that time, and one weekend I went to our condo to spend the weekend alone—and to "have it out" with God. One morning, I got up early and went for a walk on the beach. There were a few people beginning to set up for the day, but overall it was still quiet. The sun was coming up and the waves were crashing gently on the shore. It was absolutely beautiful, and very peaceful—just what I needed. I have no idea how long I walked and prayed, but I will never ever forget what happened that morning.

As I walked, I remember looking at all the footsteps in the sand. There were large man-size footprints from runners and small footsteps next to larger ones from kids walking with their parents. There were footsteps everywhere. I know what I'm about to say sounds crazy, but it's my story and I'm sticking to it. I continued walking down the beach until eventually only one set of footprints was left next to mine. It was the large bare-foot print of a man—but there was no one there. Stopping dead in my tracks, I looked up and thanked God for revealing him-self to me in that moment.

Experiencing my parents' divorce was one of the toughest times I've ever gone through, and to be perfectly honest, it took several years before I felt "normal" again. My siblings scattered, and our huge family literally disintegrated. It took years to rebuild damaged relationships. But God gently showed me in different ways that he was always with me, every minute of every day.

God got us through that painful time—and one day he brought a woman named Ruth into our lives. He was still with us on that glorious day when Dad and Ruth became man and wife and promised, before God and all nineteen of their children, to love one another the rest of their lives on Earth. Through tears, I sang a song at their wedding called "Household of Faith" that perfectly described the home we all so desperately wanted. As hard as it was watching Dad go through that awful divorce, God has truly created beauty from the ashes by giving him Ruth. She's been a gift to all of us Williams kids, and she has patiently put our family back together—piece by piece by piece—and we have a *lot* of pieces! Looking back on it all, it's clear God was there every step of the way.

> *Looking back, you can always see his footprints.*

Now that I've survived a few tough seasons in my own life, I've seen firsthand God's faithfulness to provide us with encouragement *just* when we need it most to keep us going. One of my favorite songs by the group Third Day is called, "Cry Out to Jesus." The chorus ends by saying, "There is grace and forgiveness, mercy and healing. He'll meet you wherever you are; cry out to Jesus." It's true! No matter what pain you might be in, he understands. No matter how bad your life may have been in the past, he wants to forgive you and love you. All you have to do is ask him! Softly and tenderly, Jesus is calling. I hope you'll quiet your heart and hear him.

I don't know what your life has been like. Maybe you've had a great dad like I have, or maybe you've had a dad who has abused you, or maybe you've never even met your dad. I am so blessed to have two wonderful fathers—my earthly father and my Heavenly One—but I know that's not everyone's story. No matter what your life has been like, I hope you hear this message, for it is the truest truth I know: we all have a Heavenly Father who is madly in love with us. God is so crazy about us, he even came to Earth as a man and gave his life on the cross to build a bridge for us to get back to him. So no matter how far away from God you might be feeling, he is right there on the other side of that bridge, waiting for you to run into his outstretched arms. How I hope and pray you will cry out to Jesus and find his forgiveness, mercy, and healing for your own life.

Your story and mine are no doubt very different, but in many ways they are alike. We have known both joy and pain, waves of triumph and seemingly endless seasons of drought. Here is what I have learned: No matter how dark or how long the night, morning always comes. God is there in the night and he is there in the morning. No matter how deep the valley, there is a mountain on the other side. God is on the mountain and he is in the valley, and even when you can't trace his hand, you can always trust his heart.

Did you know that the man who wrote the hymn "It Is Well with My Soul" had just lost his fortune and most of his family when he sat down to write that unforgettable song? We have to know, just as Horatio Spafford did, that God is with us, no matter the circumstances we find ourselves in. His words of reassurance inspired one of my favorite songs. It's called, "Lay It Down." Like Spafford, I've learned to lay it all down at his feet in complete surrender to my Lord, and I've learned it's the only way to live. My prayer for you is that you can learn to lay your burdens down, too. He wants us to "cast our cares on him, because he cares for us." Allow him to permeate every aspect of your life and give you a peace that will surpass all human understanding. If there's only one thing you take away from reading this book, *please* let this be it.

I'm so grateful to my dad, who has taught me when to hold on and how to let go—and *who* to hold on to through it all.

Pat's Lesson

There is a legend I've heard about the rite of passage of a male Cherokee youth. On the big night, his father takes him into the forest, sits him on a tree stump, and blindfolds him. "You must stay here all night," his father says. "You are not to cry out for help, and you are not to remove the blindfold until you feel the morning rays of sunshine. When the night is past, if you survive and do as I have told you, you will be a man. You must not tell anyone else about your experience, for each boy must go through this passage on his own. Now I am leaving you."

Terrified, the boy sits, stone still, on a tree stump. *What are those noises? Surely there are wild beasts all around, just coming to eat me up! Or what if some other person comes to do me harm?* A fierce wind blew through the forest, shaking everything around him, but the boy sat still as a stone, unmoving. Never once did he remove the blindfold.

At long last, he felt the warm and welcome rays of the sun on his shoulders. He lifted his blindfold—and saw to his surprise his father, sitting on a nearby stump. He had been watching over his son the whole night through, protecting him from harm.

In the same way, our Heavenly Father watches over his children. So why is it we tend to call on the Lord only when things are tough? When everything is going well in our lives, we want to take the credit. But when we stumble and fall over the next obstacle in the road, to whom are we crying out to help us through?

It's true! We need to recognize that God is with us in every situation—from the mountains, to the valleys, to the oceans white with foam.

When Karyn comes to me for advice, she knows I'm not relying on my own wisdom. I've made it a habit to read God's Word every day and to model that for my kids. Thanks to that habit and the trust I've built over the years from watching God bring me victoriously through trial after trial, I know exactly where to turn when life seems unfair.

As a dad, I am so pleased to know that Karyn shares my faith. I became a believer when I was nearly thirty years old, so I appreciate how much better off we are to make that decision sooner rather than later in life. Instilling our faith into our children's hearts is the most important "take away" we can hope for. Not all of my kids are walking closely with the Lord at this writing, but I have the peace of knowing I've done all I can to point the way. Parents, if your heart is breaking because of a son or daughter who has strayed, don't give up hope. God is still God and wants your child in heaven one day, even more than you do. I believe that the Hound of Heaven will dog their heels—and he won't stop nipping—until they find the true freedom that only comes with complete surrender.

Even when we have nothing else left to hold on to, I've learned that if we have the Lord, we are wealthy and secure. Over and over again in the Bible we find God saying, "I will be with you"; "I will never leave you"; and "lo, I am with you always." Does that mean that God is there when we're in trouble the same as when we're riding the big waves? Oh yes, indeed, it does.

If you love the Lord, he truly will never leave you.

In August 2007, Orlando Magic guard Jameer Nelson's dad, a welder for a tugboat company, somehow accidentally drowned in the Delaware River. Pete Nelson was just fifty-seven years old. I traveled with the Magic team to the funeral in Chester, Pennsylvania. The church was packed, and the funeral went three hours long. There was a loved man!

The highlight of the service came when Jameer's teammate Dwight Howard, our all-star player, spoke to the crowd of one thousand people. "Jameer may have lost his earthly father," Howard said, "but he will never lose his Heavenly Father." Needless to say, the church went wild. Howard's words turned the whole atmosphere from sadness into a worship service. He understands the hope of heaven and the continual presence of God in the lives of those who love him.

My question to you is this: do you have that hope? If not, I can't urge you strongly enough to do whatever it takes to get hold of it. If you are hindered by doubts and questions—get them answered. There are plenty of people who'd love nothing more than to help you take the biggest and best step of your life—the one that leads you into the arms of God. As a dad, I was thrilled to watch my infant children learn to take their first wobbly steps. But nothing has pleased me more than to see them take God's hand and choose to walk with him. No matter where you are in life, it is never too late to make that step and be able to say with Dwight Howard, "No matter who or what else I may lose, I will never lose my Heavenly Father."

None of us can imagine how much our Heavenly Father loves us, how much he cares about us, how much he thinks about us. When we are living right smack in the middle of his will and his purpose for our lives, we experience what is known as God's blessing. To have God's blessing, or favor, in your life is the ultimate way to live an impactful life on this earth. I like to say it's plugging into the power that runs the universe. And when you plug in, you are able to live up to your full potential, to maximize your moment on Earth and become the kind of person God intended you to be when he created you. As much as it is up to you, don't let him down.

THE TAKEAWAY

It's never too late to call on the Lord. He wants us to do that! Whether you're high on a mountain of success right now or floundering in the depths of the worst valley you've ever traveled through, stay close to the one who holds your future in his able hands. He knows the plans he has for you, and they are for your good!

Stay close to the Lord—he is with you on the mountain as well as in the valley.

A Final Thought
from Karyn

Throughout the process of writing this book, there's one common thread I kept coming back to. Actually two, the first being—wow, I cry a lot!

Seriously, the common message is simply this—our words are so powerful, and our tongue can either be used as a weapon or a blessing.

Parents, the power of your example cannot be measured. I mentioned my relationship with the writers of "Watching You," the multiweek, number one smash hit country song by Rodney Atkins. In my mind, that song says it all, "I've been watching you, Dad. Ain't that cool? I'm your buckaroo. *I want to be like you.*"

The fact is, I want to be just like my dad, too. But I also realize how lucky I am to actually have a dad that I want to be like. It has amazed me to realize as I've written about the lessons in this book that while several of them were said by Dad so often we could lip-synch when he spoke them, still others are things Dad said *only one time*! And five, ten, fifteen years later, they're etched in my brain like it was yesterday.

It reminds me that the words *I'm* saying every day to others—to my friends, my family, my nieces, and my nephews—are impacting *their* lives as well. It's up to me to choose what kind of legacy I'll leave. Please let the words of this book be a lesson to you—that people are watching you every day.

Parents, it may not be your own children—it may be someone else's children who are yearning for the good example of a parent. Either way, give them "good stuff" they can cling to and apply to their own lives. Young people—you never know when adults are watching you and how you can have an impact as well. The Scripture says, "Don't let anyone look down on you because you are young, but set an example for the believers in speech, in life, in love, in faith and in purity" (1 Timothy 4:12).

This is the bottom line:

- Kids—listen to your parents. They know what they're talking about.
- Parents—your children *are* watching and listening to you, even when you think you're not getting through.

So wear your seat belt, enjoy your life, and be good to people. Remember that someone somewhere is always watching you. If that's all you take away, you'll have a great life.

Thank you for allowing me to share with you the lessons that have shaped my life. I'm so proud to call my dad my mentor, my example, and my teacher—but most of all, my friend. I pray that you, too, will one day have a friend like my dad.

ABOUT THE AUTHORS

Karyn Williams is a singer/songwriter based in Nashville, Tennessee, well on her way to country glory. The firstborn daughter of NBA executive Pat Williams, Karyn learned to fend for herself early in a household with eighteen brothers and sisters. A graduate of the University of Florida, Karyn holds a B.S. in Journalism/Broadcast Communications and held the title of Miss University of Florida 2000. She finished as first runner-up in the Miss Florida pageant later that year, also winning the interview and talent portions of the competition. Her blood pumping with sheer Williams energy, Karyn is a marathon runner like her dad, having completed nine marathons so far. Don't miss her companion music to this book, "I'm Taking You With Me" (available on iTunes or by visiting www.myspace.com/karynwilliams).

Pat Williams is the father of nineteen children and grandfather to seven more—so when it comes to dispensing sage advice, he has a deep well from which to draw. The senior vice president of the NBA's Orlando Magic, Pat has spent over forty-six years in professional athletics. He's an in-demand motivational speaker with an international audience, and has authored more than fifty-five books that focus primarily on teamwork, leadership, parenting, and personal improvement. A marathon runner, devoted reader, and diehard baseball fan, Pat refuses to accept "enough." He also helps teach an adult Sunday school class at First Baptist Church of Orlando and hosts three weekly radio broadcasts. Pat and his wife, Ruth, live in Winter Park, Florida.

Peggy Matthews Rose has partnered with Pat Williams on the books *Lincoln Speaks to Leaders* (with Gene Griessman, Elevate Books, 2009) and *Read for Your Life* (2007, Health Communications, Inc.). Her background includes many years writing and editing for Disneyland and The Walt Disney Company, with her current focus on individual clients. Peggy has co-authored a children's picture book, *Tiffany and the Talking Frog in The Search for the Crown of Rye Chestnuts*, with women's ministry leader Sandra Maddox (Triumverate, 2008). Additionally, Peggy has collaborated with a pastor on two books about each person's unique purpose in life.

You can contact Pat Williams at:
Pat Williams
c/o Orlando Magic
8701 Maitland Summit Boulevard
Orlando, FL 32810
(407) 916-2404
pwilliams@orlandomagic.com

Visit Pat Williams's website at:
www.PatWilliamsMotivate.com

If you would like to set up a speaking engagement for Pat Williams, please call Andrew Herdliska at (407) 916-2401 or e-mail him at aherdliska@orlandomagic.com.

You can contact Karyn Williams at:
Karyn Williams
c/o KarynAboutMusic
KarynAboutMusic@gmail.com

Visit Karyn's website at:
www.myspace.com/karynwilliams

If you're interested in scheduling Karyn for a concert, speaking engagement, or special music for your event, contact KarynAboutMusic at (615) 568-9196 or karynaboutmusic@gmail.com.

We would love to hear from you. Please send your comments about this book to Pat and/or Karyn Williams at the above address or in care of our publisher at the address below. Thank you.

Health Communications, Inc.
3201 S. W. 15th Street
Deerfield Beach, FL 33442
Fax: (954) 360-0034

DON'T MISS KARYN'S POWERFUL SONG

"Taking You With Me," written especially for her dad
in conjunction with this book.

Available for download now on iTunes,
or visit Karyn's website for ordering instructions:
www.myspace.com/karynwilliams

WHAT OTHERS ARE SAYING ABOUT "TAKING YOU WITH ME"...

"This song is wonderful. It makes me wish
I had a daughter like Karyn!"

—**David Robinson,**
former NBA superstar

"Wow! This song is the daughter's response to Butterfly Kisses!
You're going to have to include a set of
tissues with every CD sold!"

—**Brian White,** Two-time Dove Award
winning & ACM nominated songwriter

"Pat, of all the things you've done in your life, your daughter
Karyn has to be your greatest accomplishment. You must be
so proud of this beautiful young woman and this incredibly
powerful song she has written for and about you. It's obvious
the two of you have a special bond. This song is going
to touch so many lives; its message overwhelmed me
and brought me to tears . . . wow!"

—**Stan Van Gundy,**
Head Coach, Orlando Magic

"In all of my years of ministry, I do not ever recall being so overwhelmed in worship than when Karyn sang 'Taking You With Me' before mega thousands of people. The chills are covering me for a second time as I am writing! The last verse in the Old Testament says, 'He will turn the hearts of the fathers to their children, and the hearts of the children to their fathers....' I believe with all my heart that God will use 'Taking You With Me' to restore and/or enhance many father/child relationships and I praise God He is using Karyn to carry out His will."

—**Randall James**, Chairman
Southern Baptist Convention Executive Committee

"The first time I heard 'Taking You With Me,' I was driving home from work and I had to pull over—it stopped me dead in my tracks. As the song played, I cried as I thought of my own daughter. Karyn has written a powerful song that she sure sings from her heart! I truly believe this song will spread a message of love and hope across the globe."

—**David Uth**,
Senior Pastor, First Baptist Church, Orlando